simply salads

jennifer chandler

Photographs by Langdon Clay

Ruteledge Hill Press®
Nashville, Tennessee

A Division of Thomas Nelson Publishers
www.thomasnelson.com

Published by Rutledge Hill Press, a division of Thomas Nelson, Inc., P.O. Box 141000, Nashville, Tennessee 37214.

Rutledge Hill Press books may be purchased in bulk for educational, business, fund-raising, or sales promotional use. For information, please e-mail SpecialMarkets@ThomasNelson.com.

Library of Congress Cataloging-in-Publication Data

Chandler, Jennifer, 1970-
  Simply salads / Jennifer Chandler ; photography by Langdon Clay.
     p. cm.
  Includes index.
  ISBN-13: 978-1-4016-0320-5
  ISBN-10: 1-4016-0320-3
1. Salads. I. Title.
  TX740.C3855 2007
  641.8'3--dc22

                              2006031264

Printed in China
06 07 08 09 10—5 4 3 2 1

dedicated
to
Paul, Hannah,
and Sarah

contents

preface

Packaged salad blends have changed the way I enjoy salads. With all the varieties of greens now available at the grocery store, it has never been easier to make a great and tasty salad. Dozens of pre-washed salad blends allow the home cook the ease and convenience of picking the perfect mixture for their salad without all the hassle.

I can't remember the last time I purchased a head of leaf lettuce or sifted through a big pile of wilting mesclun greens searching for the freshest ones. Specialty greens such as arugula and mache, once only enjoyed in restaurants, have found their way to my dining table.

Before bagged blends, I would have never bought four different types of lettuce just to make the perfect blend for a salad for just my husband and me. Now there are more than fifty different combinations of lettuces, packaged in just the right size, from which to choose.

Whoever decided to make these blends "ready-to-eat" was a genius in my book. Cleaning all the sand and dirt out of fresh spinach is an inconvenience I have not experienced since I found the pre-washed packaged variety. And, assuming I could find it in the back of a cabinet, I can guarantee that my salad spinner has a layer of dust on it.

To turn a simple salad into a spectacular dish, just add your favorite ingredients. The possibilities are infinite when it comes to the salad creations that you can make. Now you can try your favorite restaurant salad at home or experiment with tastes from other countries.

A salad can be so much more than just a precursor to a meal or a bland diet food. Dishes made from leafy greens can make a delicious, and healthy, main attraction of any meal. For a hearty meal, just add your favorite protein. Top the salad with a warm piece of grilled meat or fish. If you prefer a cold salad, combine shredded, chilled chicken with the greens. Toss in some of your favorite veggies, fruits, or nuts to add different tastes and textures. Crumbled or grated cheeses also make flavorful additions.

Thanks to the conveniences of the bags, I enjoy a delicious salad at home almost every day. My wish is that this book inspires you to get creative in the kitchen and eat great salads often!

Enjoy!

Introduction

These recipes are meant to be guidelines to show you how to turn a bag of greens into a spectacular dish. The beauty of composing a salad is that there really are no rules. I encourage you to make substitutions or changes to create your own original, delicious dish.

For each salad, I listed the salad blend that I thought went well with other ingredients. You can easily substitute almost any salad blend for another. Pick your favorite blends and use them. If your grocery is out of Triple Hearts salad blend, for example, pick up a bag of Hearts of Romaine instead. If Spring Mix is your absolute favorite, use it all the time.

I make my salad dressings from scratch 99 percent of the time. Why buy bottled dressing when it is so easy to make your own? A wonderful dressing can easily be whipped up in seconds. Most dressing ingredients are staples that you probably have in your kitchen right now. Homemade dressings are also a lot cheaper than the bottled versions, and there is no waste since you make only the amount you need.

Most dressing recipes in this book make enough to evenly coat the salad. Dress your salads to your taste. If you like a lightly dressed salad, don't use all the dressing. If you prefer salad with your dressing, double the recipe.

But, if you don't want to make your own dressing, don't feel guilty. Packaged salads—and all my recipes—are about conveniently putting a healthy, delicious meal on the table. Use your favorite bottled dressings—and yes, I have one I keep in the fridge for that 1 percent of the time—when you want. You may not find the exact duplicate, but you can come close to substituting every dressing in this book at your local supermarket.

The most important key to delicious salads is to use the best ingredients. Always buy the freshest produce and, when possible, use locally grown products. Invest in a good extra virgin olive oil and flavorful vinegars. Quality ingredients will ensure perfectly scrumptious salads.

salad blends 101

Convenient, healthy, and tasty. That's the simplest way to describe the phenomenon of packaged salad blends.

They are an easy way to enjoy a healthy and tasty salad—whether you are in the mood for a blend of traditional lettuces such as Romaine or iceberg or a gourmet blend of baby greens.

Since they were first introduced in the late 1980s, purchasing prewashed, precut packaged salads has become the norm. Today Americans are eating almost thirty pounds of lettuce per year; most of that comes out of a bag.

Innovative companies are doing all the hard work for us. Everything they do, from growing, harvesting, cleaning, packaging, and delivering, is designed to give us fresh salads for our tables.

From a taste perspective, the home cook can now serve exciting, restaurant-style blend salads for dinner every day.

From a health perspective, baby greens are not only delicious but more nutritious than the traditional salads made from only iceberg or romaine lettuces.

HOW TO SELECT SALAD BLENDS

Available in either bags or clamshell packaging, salad blends are stored in the refrigerated area of the supermarket's produce section.

On the front of each package, the salad is stamped with a "Best if used by" date. Even though manufacturers say the salad should still be good on that date, my experience has been that salads tend to start going bad a few days prior to that date. My general rule of thumb is to purchase salad blends with "best by" dates a minimum of three days away. For example, if the listed date is June 6, don't buy it after June 3. Ideally, try to find blends with dates at least five days out. Don't be shy about looking toward the back of the display case for fresher bags.

In addition to looking at the date, also look at the salad to make sure it appears fresh. The packaging is see-through so you can get a good look at the product. If the lettuce shows signs of aging or mishandling (such as limp or wilted leaves with brown or yellow edges or dark, slimy spots) or is excessively wet, do not purchase that package.

STORING SALAD BLENDS

Manufacturers of salad blends have developed unique packaging that helps ensure a "just-picked" freshness and crispness of salads without the use of preservatives. Salad blends should be kept refrigerated in their original bags until use. Store the bags in the refrigerator crisper or drawer.

Leftovers should be stored in the original bag in the refrigerator crisper or drawer. For best results, squeeze out excess air and seal tightly.

Once opened, the salad should be eaten within two days.

TO WASH OR NOT

There is a big debate about whether to wash the salad blend or not.

Most salad blends are thoroughly washed, rinsed, and gently dried before packaging. Therefore, it is not necessary to wash these "ready-to-eat" salads again before eating.

If you prefer, rinsing your salad again will not damage the lettuce in any way.

SALADS BLENDS USED IN THIS BOOK

 **Hearts of Romaine:** Crisp, inner romaine leaves

 **Baby Spinach:** Tender baby spinach leaves

 **Baby Arugula:** Baby arugula leaves

 **Spring Mix:** Baby lettuces (such as baby green and red romaine, tango, baby green and red oak, lolla rosa, baby green and red leaf, and baby green and red butter), baby greens (such as red swiss chard, mizuna, tatsoi, baby spinach, and baby arugula), frisee, and radicchio

 **Fresh Herb Salad:** Baby red romaine, royal red oak, lolla rosa, new red fire, red leaf, tango, little gem, green romaine, green oak, green leaf, mizuna, tatsoi, red mustard, green mustard, red chard, green chard, arugula, spinach, radicchio, frisee, dill, and flat parsley

 **European:** Romaine, iceberg, endive, radicchio, and green leaf lettuces

 **Romaine Hearts:** Tender whole romaine hearts, tough outer leaves removed

 **Triple Hearts™:** Romaine, green leaf, and butter lettuces

 Riviera™: Butter lettuce and radicchio

 Just Lettuce®: Romaine and iceberg lettuces

 Sweet Baby Greens: Baby lettuces such as baby red and green butter lettuces, baby green and red romaine, tango, baby green and red oak, lolla rosa, and baby green and red leaf

 Lettuce Trio: Iceberg, romaine, and green leaf lettuces

 American: Romaine, iceberg, radishes, red cabbage, and shredded carrots

 Mâche Rosettes: Small bunches of mache leaves

 Italian: Romaine lettuce and radicchio

 Shredded Lettuce: Shredded iceberg lettuce

 Leafy Romaine: Romaine and leaf lettuces

Asian Salad Blend: Iceberg, romaine, red cabbage, shredded carrots, and pea pods

Shredded Carrots: Shredded carrots

Field Greens: Leaf lettuces, curly endive, radicchio, and shredded carrots

3-Color Deli Cole Slaw: Deli-cut green and red cabbage and shredded carrots

Mediterranean: Escarole, leaf lettuces, radicchio, and endive

Classic Slaw: Finely shredded green cabbage and shredded carrots

Angel Hair Slaw: Delicate strands of finely shredded green cabbage

Shredded Red Cabbage: Shredded red cabbage

Broccoli Slaw: Shredded hearts of broccoli, carrots, and red cabbage

Keeping a well-stocked kitchen will make salad preparation an ease. Here's a list of a few items that are always on hand in my kitchen.

If you have this basic list of kitchen utensils and ingredients on hand, you will effortlessly be able to make almost every salad in this book—as well as be prepared to whip up a salad on short notice.

Basic Kitchen Utensils

A salad bowl (of course!)

Mixing bowls (both large and small)

A set of graduated, straight-edge measuring
    cups made for dry ingredients

A set of measuring spoons

A glass liquid measuring cup

A small whisk

Salad tongs

Good, sharp knives (a small paring knife
    and a 6 to 8-inch chef knife are a must)

Cutting boards (at least two)

A peppermill

A large ovenproof skillet (I prefer cast iron)

8-quart stock pot

2-quart sauce pan

Baking dishes (one 8 x 8-inch and
    one 13 x 9-inch)

Large rimmed baking sheet

A colander

Vegetable peeler (the rubber
    handled ones are easier on your hands)

Traditional four-sided
    cheese grater

A blender or food processor

Can opener

Resealable containers (several for leftovers)
    and baggies

Pantry Items	Perishable/Refrigerator Items
Kosher salt	A bag of your favorite salad blend
Black peppercorns for your peppermill	Mayonnaise
Extra virgin olive oil	Sour cream
Vegetable or canola oil	Reduced-fat buttermilk
Toasted sesame oil	Garlic
Red balsamic vinegar	Parmigiano-Reggiano (Parmesan) cheese
White balsamic vinegar	Maytag blue cheese
Red wine vinegar	Red onions
White wine or champagne vinegar	Lemons and limes
Rice wine vinegar	Red bell peppers
Dijon mustard	Fresh herbs (i.e. basil, cilantro, or flat-leaf parsley)
Whole-grain Dijon mustard	Pine nuts
Soy sauce	Your favorite bottled salad dressing (for the days you feel like taking a short cut!)
Worcestershire sauce	
Granulated sugar	
Light and dark brown sugars	

greens

steakhouse wedge salad
with bacon, tomatoes, and blue cheese

Who says you can't have restaurant food at home? This version of the classic wedge salad is just as tasty as any of those served at America's top steakhouses. **Makes 6 dinner salads**

salad . . . .

1	bag (3 pack) Romaine Hearts
2	large tomatoes, diced
1	red onion, finely diced
½	pound bacon (about 10 slices), cooked, drained, and crumbled
1¼	cups crumbled blue cheese (preferably Maytag) Freshly ground black pepper

• Cut the Romaine hearts in half lengthwise. Place one wedge on each plate. Generously drizzle with the dressing. Top with the tomatoes, red onion, bacon, and blue cheese. Season with freshly ground pepper. Serve immediately.

chunky blue cheese dressing . . . .

½	cup mayonnaise
1	tablespoon minced yellow onion
½	teaspoon minced garlic
¼	cup sour cream
½	tablespoon freshly squeezed lemon juice
1	tablespoon white wine vinegar
½	cup crumbled blue cheese (preferably Maytag)
3	tablespoons reduced-fat buttermilk Kosher salt and freshly ground pepper

• In a small bowl whisk the mayonnaise, onion, garlic, sour cream, lemon juice, vinegar, blue cheese, and buttermilk together. Season with salt and pepper to taste. **Makes about 1½ cups**

tip There is no substitute for freshly cooked bacon. Use either the traditional pork or turkey variety; but avoid the temptation to use processed bacon bits.

For a lighter version, substitute balsamic vinaigrette for the chunky blue cheese dressing.

asian salad
with ponzu ginger dressing and wasabi peas

Inspired by my favorite sushi bar's house salad, this bed of greens gets its kick from wasabi peas and a tangy ponzu ginger dressing. Wasabi peas are available in most gourmet markets and specialty stores in the Asian foods section.
MAKES 6 APPETIZER OR SIDE SALADS

salad . . . .

1	bag (5 ounces) Spring Mix
1	cup wasabi peas

• In a large salad bowl, toss together the Spring Mix and wasabi peas. Add the dressing to taste and gently toss. Serve immediately.

ponzu ginger dressing . . . .

1/4	cup soy sauce
2	tablespoons water
1	tablespoon rice wine vinegar
1	tablespoon freshly squeezed lime juice
½	teaspoon grated freshly peeled ginger
1	scallion, thinly sliced

• In a small bowl whisk together the soy sauce, water, vinegar, lime juice, ginger, and scallion.
MAKES ABOUT ½ CUP

tip Toss the wasabi peas with the dressing just before serving to keep the peas crunchy.

arugula with shaved parmesan

This light and refreshing salad has Italy written all over it. I just love the peppery zing of fresh arugula. For some added crunch, sprinkle toasted pine nuts over the salad. **MAKES 6 APPETIZER OR SIDE SALADS**

salad . . . .

1	block (4 ounces) Parmesan cheese
1	package (5 ounces) Baby Arugula
	Freshly ground black pepper

• Using a vegetable peeler, shave the block of Parmesan into thin strips.

• Place the Baby Arugula in a large salad bowl. Add the vinaigrette to taste and gently toss. Season with pepper. Garnish with the shaved Parmesan. Serve immediately.

white balsamic vinaigrette . . . .

2	tablespoons white balsamic vinegar
6	tablespoons extra virgin olive oil
	A pinch of kosher salt
	Freshly ground black pepper

• Place the vinegar in a small bowl. Slowly add the oil in a stream, whisking to emulsify. Season with salt and pepper to taste. MAKES ABOUT ¼ CUP

tip It's worth the extra expense to use good, aged Parmesan cheese or even the real Italian aged Parmigiano-Reggiano rather than the processed grocery store variety. The thin strips add texture as well as a sharp, tangy taste.

wilted spinach salad

My neighbor and good friend, Ashley Woodman, invented this sweet, egg-y dressing. Whenever she serves it, her guests always ask for the recipe—like I did! MAKES 4 APPETIZER OR SIDE SALADS

salad . . . .

1	bag (6 ounces) Baby Spinach
¾	cup button mushrooms, cleaned, ends trimmed, and thinly sliced

• In a large salad bowl, place the spinach and mushrooms. Pour the hot dressing over the spinach and mushrooms and toss gently. Serve immediately.

dressing . . . .

3	tablespoons extra virgin olive oil
2	tablespoons red wine vinegar
1	small garlic clove, minced
¼	teaspoon dried tarragon
½	teaspoon kosher salt
⅛	teaspoon freshly ground pepper
1	tablespoon sugar
1	egg, cracked into a small bowl

• In a small saucepan bring the oil, vinegar, garlic, tarragon, salt, pepper, and sugar to a simmer. Add the egg and whisk with a fork until the egg is opaque and stringy and cooked through all the way.
MAKES ABOUT ⅓ CUP

tip Since this salad should be served immediately after it is tossed with the dressing, wait to make it until everything else on your menu is ready.

warm goat cheese salad
with grainy mustard vinaigrette

When I lived in Paris, this was my favorite lunchtime treat. For a nuttier version, substitute ground walnuts for the bread crumbs. **MAKES 4 DINNER SALADS**

salad ....

1	tablespoon olive oil
1	large egg
	Kosher salt and freshly ground pepper
1½	cups plain bread crumbs
1	log (10.5 ounces) fresh goat cheese, chilled in the refrigerator
1	bag (10 ounces) European Blend

• Position an oven rack to the highest setting. Preheat the oven to 395°F. Brush a baking sheet with the oil; set aside.

• In a small bowl whisk the egg with a pinch of salt and pepper. In another small bowl place the bread crumbs. Slice the goat cheese log into 8 equal pieces. Working in batches, dip the goat cheese rounds in the egg mixture, shaking off the excess. Press into the breadcrumb mixture and pat gently to evenly coat. Arrange on the prepared baking sheet.

• Place the baking sheet on the top rack of the oven and bake the goat cheese rounds until crisp and golden, about 5 minutes.

• Place the European Blend in a large salad bowl. Add the vinaigrette to taste and gently toss. Divide the salad among individual plates. Top each salad with 2 warm goat cheese rounds. Serve immediately.

grainy mustard vinaigrette ....

2	tablespoons white wine vinegar
1	tablespoon whole-grain Dijon mustard
6	tablespoons extra virgin olive oil
	Kosher salt and freshly ground pepper

• Combine the vinegar and mustard in a small bowl and whisk together. Slowly add the oil in a stream, whisking to emulsify. Season with salt and pepper to taste. **MAKES ABOUT ¼ CUP**

tip Every oven is a little different. Gas ovens cook faster than electric. If you are not familiar with your oven, please watch closely to ensure even browning.

southern caesar salad
with roasted garlic dressing

Italy meets the Old South! Popular in the South, grits are stone-ground dried kernels of corn. Traditionally served for breakfast, grits can also be served as a side dish or part of a main course. Polenta is the appropriate substitute. MAKES 4 DINNER OR 6 APPETIZER SALADS

salad . . . .

1	bag (10 ounces) Hearts of Romaine
½	cup shredded Parmesan cheese
¼	pound country ham, sliced and cut into thin strips

• In a large salad bowl, toss the Hearts of Romaine and Parmesan cheese. Add the dressing to taste and gently toss. Divide the salad among individual plates. Top with the sliced ham and grits croutons. Serve immediately.

grits croutons . . . .

1	tablespoon extra virgin olive oil
3	cups water
	Pinch of kosher salt
¾	cup stone-ground yellow grits
2	tablespoons unsalted butter
	Vegetable oil for frying

• Lightly grease bottom and sides of an 8 x 8-inch baking pan with the oil. Set aside.

• Bring the water to a boil in a medium pot. Whisk in the salt and grits. Simmer, stirring occasionally, until the mixture thickens and the grits are tender, about 15 minutes. Remove from the heat, add the butter, and stir until melted.

• Pour the hot grits into the prepared pan, spreading evenly to about ¾ inch thick. Refrigerate until cold and firm, about 2 hours.

• Once cooled, cut the grits into ¾-inch cubes. Fill a heavy large frying pan with vegetable oil until it is about 1-inch deep. Over medium-high heat, warm the oil until a few water droplets sizzle in pan. Working in small batches, carefully add the grits cubes to the hot oil one at a time and fry until golden, about 2 minutes. Using a slotted spoon, transfer the croutons to a paper towel–lined plate to drain and cool.

tip   The Grits Croutons can be prepared one day ahead if stored in an airtight container.

roasted garlic dressing ....

2	heads garlic
⅓	cup plus 1 tablespoon extra virgin olive oil
	Kosher salt and freshly ground pepper
2	tablespoons freshly squeezed lemon juice
1	tablespoon Dijon mustard
1	teaspoon anchovy paste
1	teaspoon Worcestershire sauce

• Preheat the oven to 300°F. Trim about ½ inch off the top of the heads of garlic, leaving the heads intact. Place the garlic in a small casserole dish.

• Drizzle 1 tablespoon of the olive oil over the cut top of the garlic. Season with salt and pepper. Cover with aluminum foil and bake until the garlic is soft, about 1½ hours. Set aside to cool.

• Squeeze the base of the garlic to remove the cloves from the skin. Transfer the garlic to a blender. Add the lemon juice, mustard, anchovy paste, and Worcestershire sauce. Purée the mixture until smooth. With the machine running, slowly add the remaining ⅓ cup oil in a stream. Season with salt and pepper to taste.

MAKES ABOUT ½ CUP

confetti chip salad

I have to admit I thought my friend was crazy when she shared her recipe for a salad tossed with chips. But what a great texture and flavor these chips give to lettuce! **MAKES 6 APPETIZER OR SIDE SALADS**

salad

1	bag (10 ounces) Hearts of Romaine
½	red bell pepper, seeded and diced
½	yellow bell pepper, seeded and diced
1	ripe avocado, peeled and diced
1	cup multicolor vegetable chips, such as Terra Chip Stix

• In a large salad bowl, toss together the Hearts of Romaine, red bell pepper, yellow bell pepper, avocado, and vegetable chips. Add the dressing to taste and gently toss. Serve immediately.

dressing

¼	cup vegetable oil
¼	cup red wine vinegar
2	tablespoons sugar
1	tablespoon ketchup
	Kosher salt and freshly ground pepper

• In a small bowl whisk together the oil, vinegar, sugar, and ketchup until the sugar has dissolved. Season with salt and pepper to taste. **MAKES ABOUT ½ CUP**

tip Available in most grocery stores, Terra Chips are chips made from colorful root vegetables. Fried potato sticks make a tasty, but not as colorful, substitute.

spinach salad
with roasted cherry tomatoes

Roasting tomatoes takes hardly any effort and provides a sweet and intense flavor to this classic salad.
MAKES 6 APPETIZER OR SIDE SALADS

salad . . . .

1	pint cherry or grape tomatoes, halved
2	tablespoons extra virgin olive oil
	Kosher salt and freshly ground pepper
1	bag (6 ounces) Baby Spinach
½	red onion, halved and thinly sliced
1	cup shredded blue cheese (preferably Maytag)

• Preheat the oven to 450°F. Place the tomato halves, skin side down, in a roasting pan or on a baking sheet with sides. Drizzle the oil over the tomatoes and season with salt and pepper. Roast, shaking the pan after the first 10 minutes to prevent sticking, until shriveled and moist tender, about 20 minutes. Remove from the oven and cool to room temperature, about 15 minutes.

• In a large salad bowl, toss the spinach with the red onion. Add the vinaigrette to taste and gently toss. Divide salad among individual plates. Top with the roasted tomatoes and blue cheese. Serve immediately.

balsamic dijon vinaigrette . . . .

2	tablespoons balsamic vinegar
1	teaspoon Dijon mustard
6	tablespoons extra virgin olive oil
	Kosher salt and freshly ground pepper

• Place the vinegar and mustard in a small bowl and whisk together. Slowly add the oil in a stream, whisking to emulsify. Season with salt and pepper to taste. MAKES ABOUT ¼ CUP

tip Maytag Blue Cheese has been deemed the best American blue cheese. Store bought crumbles and other grocery brands can't hold a candle to its rich creamy flavor and texture. Luckily, Maytag Blue Cheese is now available in the gourmet cheese section of most neighborhood grocery stores. It is well worth the effort to find it.

classic spinach salad
with bacon, red onion, and hard-boiled eggs

Enjoy this hearty salad as the main attraction with a cup of tomato soup on the side.

MAKES 4 DINNER OR 6 APPETIZER SALADS

salad . . . .

1	bag (6 ounces) Baby Spinach
½	red onion, halved and thinly sliced
4	hard-boiled eggs, peeled and quartered
12	bacon slices, cooked and drained
6	button mushrooms, thinly sliced

• Divide the Baby Spinach among individual plates. Drizzle with the dressing to taste. Top with the onion, eggs, bacon slices, and mushrooms. Serve immediately.

creamy garlic dressing . . . .

1	small garlic clove, minced
5	teaspoons red wine vinegar
2	teaspoons honey
4	tablespoons mayonnaise
2	tablespoons extra virgin olive oil
	Kosher salt and freshly ground pepper

• Place the garlic, vinegar, honey, mayonnaise, and oil in a blender or food processor. Purée until smooth. Season with salt and pepper to taste.

MAKES ABOUT ½ CUP

tip To make the perfect hard-boiled egg, place the egg in a small saucepan and cover with water. Bring to a boil. Remove from the heat, cover, and set aside for 12 minutes. Drain and peel the egg.

classic caesar salad
with herb croutons

Using whole anchovies and egg, this dressing is close to the original version invented by Caesar Cardini back in 1924 at his Italian Restaurant in Tijuana, Mexico. The herb croutons, which my good friend Lisa Toporek created, complement this flavorful salad. MAKES 6 APPETIZER SALADS

salad . . . .

1	bag (10 ounces) Hearts of Romaine
½	cup shredded Parmesan cheese

• In a large bowl toss together the Hearts of Romaine, Parmesan cheese, and Herb Croutons. Add the dressing to taste and gently toss. Serve immediately.

herb croutons . . . .

6	tablespoons salted butter, melted
2	teaspoons garlic powder
2	tablespoons dried Italian herbs
½	loaf (15 ounces) French bread, cut into 1-inch cubes

• Preheat the oven to 375°F. In a small bowl stir together the melted butter, garlic powder, and Italian herbs. Place the cubes of bread in a large bowl. Spoon the butter mixture over the bread cubes; toss to evenly coat. In a single layer, spread the bread cubes on a rimmed baking sheet. Bake, turning the pan as needed, until golden brown, about 10 to 15 minutes. Set aside to cool to room temperature.

caesar dressing . . . .

2	small garlic cloves, mashed to a paste (see tip on page 230 for instructions) or minced
2	anchovy fillets, minced, or ½ teaspoon anchovy paste
1	egg (see Tip below), cracked into a small bowl
2	tablespoons freshly squeezed lemon juice
1	tablespoon Dijon mustard
¼	teaspoon Worcestershire sauce

½	cup extra virgin olive oil
	Kosher salt and freshly ground pepper

• In a small bowl whisk together the garlic, anchovies, egg, lemon juice, mustard, and Worcestershire sauce. Add the oil in a stream, whisking until the dressing is emulsified. Season with salt and pepper to taste.
MAKES ABOUT ¾ CUP

tip Because it has a raw egg in it, this dressing must be refrigerated and used the same day it is made. If you are wary of serving a dressing with a raw egg, substitute 1 tablespoon mayonnaise or try the Roasted Garlic Dressing on page 13.

hot chili oil salad

Hot yet refreshing! The fresh herbs, jicama, and strawberries cool the heat of the chili oil.

MAKES 6 APPETIZER OR SIDE SALADS

salad

1	bag (5 ounces) Spring Mix
1	red onion, sliced into thin rings
1	pint strawberries, hulled and thinly sliced
1	small jicama, peeled and cut into matchsticks
½	cup toasted pepitas (pumpkin seeds)

• In a large salad bowl, toss together the Spring Mix, onion, strawberries, jicama, and pepitas. Add the dressing to taste and gently toss. Serve immediately.

hot chili oil vinaigrette

2	tablespoons raspberry balsamic vinegar
4	teaspoons freshly squeezed lemon juice
1	teaspoon Dijon mustard
¼	teaspoon ground cumin
¼	cup extra-virgin olive oil
1	tablespoon hot chili oil
¾	teaspoon minced fresh basil
¾	teaspoon minced fresh rosemary
¾	teaspoon minced fresh oregano
¾	teaspoon minced fresh mint leaves
	Kosher salt and freshly ground black pepper

• In a small bowl whisk together the vinegar, lemon juice, mustard, and cumin. Slowly add the olive oil and chili oil in a steady stream, whisking to emulsify. Stir in the basil, rosemary, oregano, and mint just before serving. Season with salt and pepper to taste.
MAKES ABOUT ½ CUP

tip Jicama is a subtly sweet, crunchy root vegetable originally found only in Mexico and South America. It is seasonally available in many grocery stores. Ask your produce department to order it for you.

A crunchy treat from Mexico, pepitas are green hulled pumpkin seeds. They are available in health food stores as well as gourmet and Latin markets.

grilled romaine
with green goddess dressing

Slightly grilling the romaine gives it an unforgettably delicious smoky flavor. MAKES 6 APPETIZER SALADS

salad ....

1	bag (3 pack) Romaine Hearts
4	tablespoons extra-virgin olive oil
	Kosher salt and freshly ground pepper
1	cup drained Mandarin orange slices (available jarred or canned)
½	cup almond slices, toasted

• Heat a clean grill to medium high. Cut the Romaine Hearts in half lengthwise. Brush the romaine with the oil and season with salt and pepper to taste. Grill, turning frequently, until slightly charred but not heated all the way through, about 5 minutes.

• Place the grilled romaine on plates. Drizzle with the dressing to taste and garnish with the Mandarin oranges and almond slices. Serve immediately.

green goddess dressing ....

1	ripe avocado, peeled and diced
⅓	cup reduced-fat buttermilk
¼	cup fresh flat-leaf parsley leaves
2	tablespoons mayonnaise
2	tablespoons thinly sliced fresh chives
¼	teaspoon minced garlic

2	tablespoons freshly squeezed lemon juice
	Kosher salt and freshly ground pepper

• In a blender purée the avocado, buttermilk, parsley, mayonnaise, chives, garlic, and lemon juice. Season to taste with salt and pepper. MAKES ABOUT ¾ CUP

tip Because of the avocado in this dressing, make this no more than one hour ahead of time. To help keep the vibrant green color, gently press plastic wrap over the surface of the dressing so that it will not oxidize.

If you prefer a thinner dressing, blend 1 to 2 tablespoons room temperature water, adding just a little at a time, into the dressing until the desired consistency is reached. Take note: you can always add more water, but you can not take it out.

wild flower herb salad

Bright and cheery, this wild flower salad is the perfect starter for a bridesmaid luncheon or baby shower.
MAKES 4 TO 6 SIDE SALADS

salad . . . .

1	bag (5 ounces) Fresh Herb blend
½	cup toasted sunflowers seeds
4	tablespoons finely sliced chives
1	cup edible flowers (nasturtiums, marigolds, and/or pansies)

• In a large salad bowl, toss together the Fresh Herb blend, sunflower seeds, and chives. Add the vinaigrette to taste and gently toss. Arrange the whole flowers on the salad. Serve immediately.

champagne vinaigrette . . . .

2	tablespoons champagne vinegar
1	shallot, minced
6	tablespoons extra virgin olive oil
	Kosher salt and freshly ground pepper

• In a small bowl whisk together the vinegar and shallots. Slowly add the oil in a steady stream, whisking to emulsify. Season with salt and pepper to taste. MAKES ABOUT ¼ CUP

tip Edible flowers are available at gourmet markets, specialty spice stores, and farmers' markets. Or if you feel like picking your own, be sure to refer to an edible flower guide since not all flowers can be eaten.

CHAPTER TWO

poultry

chinese chicken salad
with peanut dressing

Peanut butter lovers beware. The dressing in this colorful and tasty salad is addictive. **MAKES 4 DINNER SALADS**

½   cup Peanut Dressing (see page 234)
½   cup fresh snow peas
1   bag (5 ounces) Spring Mix
2   cups shredded cooked chicken
2   carrots, peeled and grated
¼   cup thinly sliced scallions
¼   cup fresh cilantro leaves
½   cup chopped roasted peanuts
2   limes, quartered, for garnish

• Prepare the Peanut Dressing.

• Bring salted water to a boil in a medium pot. Add the snow peas and cook until vibrant green and crisp tender, 1 to 1½ minutes. Drain the snow peas and immerse in an ice water bath to stop the cooking process. Drain again and place in a large salad bowl.

• Add the Spring Mix, chicken, carrots, scallions, cilantro, and peanuts and toss. Add the dressing to taste and gently toss to coat.

• Garnish with lime wedges. Serve immediately.

tip To save time, pick up a roasted rotisserie chicken at your local grocery for this recipe. The meat will be fresh, juicy, and flavorful.

mandarin chicken salad
with toasted sesame vinaigrette

Fresh greens, juicy Mandarin oranges, crunchy Ramen noodles, tasty cashews, and sesame vinaigrette make this Asian salad sure to please. MAKES 4 DINNER SALADS

salad . . . .

4	skinless, boneless chicken breasts
½	cup Teriyaki sauce
	Kosher salt and freshly ground pepper
1	bag (5 ounces) Spring Mix
½	cup drained Mandarin orange slices (available jarred or canned)
½	red onion, halved and thinly sliced
½	cup roasted, unsalted cashew nuts
¾	package (3 ounces) Oriental flavor Ramen noodles, lightly broken

• Place the chicken breasts in a large bowl and coat with the Teriyaki sauce. Cover, refrigerate, and marinate about 30 minutes.

• Heat a clean grill to medium high. Remove the chicken from the marinade, shaking off the excess, and season with salt and pepper. Discard the marinade. Grill until no longer pink in the middle, 6 to 8 minutes per side. Remove the chicken from the grill and set aside to cool to room temperature. Once cooled, cut into ½-inch pieces.

• Toss the Spring Mix with the chicken, Mandarin oranges, red onion, cashew nuts, and Ramen noodles. Add the dressing to taste and gently toss to coat. Serve immediately.

toasted sesame vinaigrette . . . .

2	tablespoons toasted sesame oil
2	tablespoons vegetable oil
5	teaspoons sugar
3	tablespoons rice wine vinegar
	Kosher salt and freshly ground pepper

• Combine the sesame oil, vegetable oil, sugar, and vinegar into a small bowl. Whisk until the sugar has dissolved. Season with salt and pepper to taste. MAKES ABOUT ¼ CUP

tip For a crunchier texture, substitute Angel Hair Cole Slaw for the Spring Mix.

black and blue chicken salad

Black and Blue in the good sense! Tangy blue cheese is a great complement for the spicy blackened chicken in this salad. MAKES 4 DINNER SALADS

¼	cup Balsamic Dijon Vinaigrette (see page 16)
4	skinless, boneless chicken breasts
4	tablespoons blackening seasoning
1	bag (5 ounces) Spring Mix
2	Roma tomatoes, diced
1	cup crumbled blue cheese

• Prepare the Balsamic Dijon Vinaigrette and set aside.

• Heat a clean grill to medium-high. Season both sides of the chicken with the blackening seasoning. Grill until no longer pink in the middle, 6 to 8 minutes per side. Remove the chicken from the grill and let rest for 5 minutes. Slice thinly against the grain.

• In a large salad bowl, toss the Spring Mix with the vinaigrette to taste. Divide the salad among individual plates. Top with the tomatoes, blue cheese, and sliced chicken. Serve immediately.

tip If you don't own a grill, warm 1 tablespoon olive oil in a cast iron or heavy ovenproof skillet until a few water droplets sizzle in pan. Sear the chicken until well browned on all sides, about 2 minutes per side, and then bake in a 395°F oven until no longer pink in the middle, about 10 minutes.

margarita chicken salad
with pepitas, cranberries, and cojita cheese

Automatic Slim's Tonga Club is one of my favorite restaurants in Memphis, Tennessee. This is my rendition of one of the many great salads that Chef Karen Blockman Carrier serves there. **MAKES 4 DINNER SALADS**

salad . . . .

½	cup freshly squeezed lime juice
¼	cup freshly squeezed orange juice
¼	cup tequila
1	tablespoon chili powder
½	fresh jalapeño, seeded and minced
2	small garlic cloves, minced
4	boneless, skinless chicken breasts
	Kosher salt and freshly ground black pepper
1	bag (5 ounces) Spring Mix
½	cup toasted pepitas (pumpkin seeds)
½	cup dried cranberries
2	tangerines, peeled, sectioned, and seeded
1	cup crumbled Cojita Mexican cheese

• In a large bowl mix together the lime juice, orange juice, tequila, chili powder, jalapeño, and garlic. Add

citrus dressing . . . .

3	tablespoons freshly squeezed lime juice
2	tablespoons freshly squeezed orange juice
2	teaspoons sugar
3	tablespoons canola oil
	Kosher salt and freshly ground pepper

the chicken breasts and toss to coat. Cover and refrigerate for 2 to 6 hours.

• Heat a clean grill to medium high. Remove the chicken from the marinade, shaking off the excess, and season both sides with salt and pepper to taste. Discard the marinade. Grill until no longer pink in the middle, 6 to 8 minutes per side. Remove the chicken from the grill and let rest for 5 minutes. Slice thinly against the grain.

• In a large salad bowl, toss together the Spring Mix, pepitas, cranberries, tangerine sections, and cheese. Add the dressing to taste and gently toss to coat. Divide the salad among individual plates. Top with the sliced chicken. Serve immediately.

• In a small bowl whisk together the lime juice, orange juice, sugar, and oil until the sugar has dissolved. Season with salt and pepper to taste. MAKES ABOUT ⅓ CUP

Cojita is a firm, salty cheese from Mexico. If you can't find it at your local market, Feta cheese is a substitute.

cobb salad
with buttermilk garlic dressing

Who would have ever imagined that one of America's most famous salads would have been invented by a hungry restaurant manager making a quick bite to eat using leftovers?! Thank goodness that Bob Cobb of the Brown Derby Restaurant in Hollywood was resourceful or we wouldn't have this delicious salad today.

MAKES 4 DINNER SALADS

salad . . . .

1	bag (8 ounces) Triple Hearts™
1½	cups cooked chicken (baked or grilled), chilled and cut into 1-inch cubes
½	pound bacon (about 10 slices), cooked and crumbled
6	hard-boiled eggs, peeled and diced
6	Roma tomatoes, seeded and diced
1	cup crumbled blue cheese (preferably Maytag)
2	ripe avocados, peeled and diced

• Place the Triple Hearts in a large salad bowl. Add the dressing to taste and gently toss. Divide the salad among individual plates. In rows, top the salad with the chicken, bacon, eggs, tomatoes, blue cheese, and avocados. Serve immediately.

buttermilk garlic dressing . . . .

½	cup sour cream
½	cup mayonnaise
¼	teaspoon minced garlic
¼	teaspoon paprika
½	teaspoon dry mustard
1	tablespoon sugar
¼	cup reduced-fat buttermilk
	Kosher salt and freshly ground pepper

• Place the sour cream, mayonnaise, garlic, paprika, dry mustard, sugar, and buttermilk in a blender. Blend until the sugar has dissolved and the dressing is smooth. Season with salt and pepper to taste.

MAKES ABOUT 1¼ CUPS

tip   When making the dressing, be sure to purée the ingredients in a blender to fully incorporate that wonderful garlic flavor into the dressing.

jalapeño chicken salad
with avocado dressing

With only the guidelines of mixing cooked chicken with a dressing and your favorite ingredients, the sky's the limit on what can compose your favorite chicken salad recipe. I like the kick that this version gets from diced jalapeños.
MAKES 4 DINNER SALADS

salad . . . .

3	skinless, boneless chicken breasts
4	tablespoons mayonnaise
2	teaspoons finely grated lime zest
2	tablespoons finely chopped shallots
2	tablespoons finely chopped seeded red bell pepper
1	teaspoon chopped seeded fresh jalapeño
1	ripe avocado, peeled and diced
	Kosher salt and freshly ground pepper
1	bag (7 ounces) Riviera™ Blend

• Bring a large saucepan of salted water to boil. Add the chicken breasts. Reduce the heat to medium-low, cover, and gently simmer until the chicken is until no longer pink in the middle, about 12 minutes. Transfer to a plate to cool. When cool enough to handle, chop the chicken into ½-inch cubes.

• In a large bowl combine the mayonnaise, lime zest, shallots, red bell pepper, and jalapeño. Fold the chicken into the mayonnaise mixture to coat. Gently stir in the diced avocado. Season with salt and pepper to taste.

• Place the Riviera Blend in a large salad bowl. Add the dressing to taste and gently toss. Divide the salad among individual plates. Top with a generous scoop of the chicken salad.

avocado vinaigrette . . . .

3	tablespoons vegetable oil
5	tablespoons freshly squeezed lime juice
¼	cup sour cream
1	ripe avocado, peeled and diced
2	to 3 tablespoons room temperature water
	Kosher salt and freshly ground pepper

• Place the oil, lime juice, sour cream, and avocado in a blender. Blend until smooth. Thin with room temperature water as needed. Season with salt and pepper to taste. MAKES ABOUT ¾ CUP

tip Using freshly squeezed lime or lemon juice in a dressing adds a light citrus taste to the salad.

chicken stir-fry salad

Skip the rice and use greens instead for a light and flavorful rendition of chicken stir-fry. **MAKES 4 DINNER SALADS**

salad . . . .

1	tablespoon vegetable oil
3	skinless, boneless chicken breasts, cut into ⅓-inch cubes
	Kosher salt and freshly ground pepper
¼	cup fresh basil leaves, thinly sliced
¼	cup chopped roasted peanuts
1	tablespoon peeled and grated fresh ginger
1	bag (6 ounces) Baby Spinach
½	bag (16 ounces) Broccoli Slaw
1	cucumber, halved lengthwise, seeded, and thinly sliced
1	red bell pepper, seeded and sliced into thin strips

• In a wok over medium-high heat, warm the oil until a few water droplets sizzle in pan. Season the chicken with salt and pepper. Place the chicken in the wok and cook, stirring occasionally, until well browned and no longer pink in the middle, 6 to 8 minutes. Remove the wok from the heat and add the basil, peanuts, ginger, and half of the dressing. Toss to coat.

• In a large salad bowl, toss the Baby Spinach, Broccoli Slaw, cucumber, and red bell pepper. Add the remaining dressing to taste and gently toss.

• Divide the salad among individual plates. Top with the warm chicken mixture. Serve immediately.

asian sesame dressing . . . .

⅓	cup freshly squeezed orange juice
1	teaspoon toasted sesame oil
2	tablespoons soy sauce
1	teaspoon light brown sugar
¼	teaspoon Asian garlic chili paste
1	tablespoon freshly squeezed lime juice
1	small garlic clove, minced
2	tablespoons vegetable oil
	Kosher salt and freshly ground pepper

• In a small bowl whisk together the orange juice, sesame oil, soy sauce, brown sugar, chili paste, lime juice, garlic, and vegetable oil until the sugar has dissolved. Season with salt and pepper to taste. MAKES ABOUT ½ CUP

tip To seed a cucumber, first cut it in half lengthwise and then scoop out the seeds with a spoon. Whether or not to peel a cucumber totally depends on your preference; however, the cucumber should be peeled before cutting it.

southern fried chicken salad

Marinating chicken in buttermilk is the Southern way to prepare fried chicken. Top this diner-style salad with fried chicken fingers from your local store if you are in a hurry. MAKES 4 DINNER SALADS

salad . . . .

3	skinless, boneless chicken breasts, cut into 12 chicken tenders
1½	cups reduced-fat buttermilk
1½	cups all-purpose flour
1	tablespoon kosher salt
1	tablespoon freshly ground black pepper
1	quart vegetable oil for frying
2	bags (12 ounces each) American Blend
8	hard-boiled eggs, peeled and halved
2	tomatoes, cut into 8 wedges each
8	baby dill pickles, halved lengthwise

• Place the chicken tenders in a large bowl. Add the buttermilk and toss to coat. Cover, refrigerate, and marinate for up to 12 hours.

• Combine the flour, salt, and pepper in a large bowl. Working in small batches, remove the chicken from the buttermilk, shaking off the excess, and place in the flour mixture. Pat gently to evenly coat. Discard the marinade.

• Pour 1-inch of oil in the bottom of a heavy stockpot. Heat to medium-high heat or until a deep-fry or candy thermometer registers 360°F. Working in small batches, carefully place the chicken tenders in the hot oil and fry until the chicken is well browned and no longer pink inside, about 15 minutes. Allow the oil to return to 360°F between batches. Place the cooked chicken strips on a rack to drain.

• Divide the American Blend among individual plates. Arrange the eggs, tomato wedges, dill pickles, and fried chicken on top. Drizzle with the dressing to taste. Serve immediately.

grainy honey mustard dressing . . . .

6	tablespoons mayonnaise	1½	tablespoons honey
2	tablespoons whole-grain Dijon mustard	2	to 3 tablespoons room temperature water
2	tablespoons Dijon mustard		Kosher salt and freshly ground pepper
2	tablespoons prepared yellow mustard		

• In a small bowl whisk together the mayonnaise, whole-grain mustard, Dijon mustard, yellow mustard, and honey. Whisk in enough water to thin the mixture to the desired consistency. Season with salt and pepper to taste. MAKES ¾ CUP

tip If the chicken is browning too quickly, lower the heat to medium-low during the cooking process or transfer browned uncooked pieces to a baking sheet and finish cooking in a 375°F oven.

bbq chicken salad
with black bean and corn salsa

Cowboys look out! This salad combines the best of the Southwest all in one dish. **Makes 4 dinner salads**

salad ....

½	cup Buttermilk Ranch Dressing (see page 232)
4	skinless, boneless chicken breasts
¾	cup your favorite BBQ sauce
	Kosher salt and freshly ground pepper
1	bag (12 ounces) American Blend
2	ripe avocados, peeled and thinly sliced
2	cups tortilla chips

• Prepare the Buttermilk Ranch Dressing.

• Place the chicken breasts in a large bowl and coat with the BBQ sauce. Cover and marinate in the refrigerator for 30 minutes.

black bean and corn salsa ....

1	can (15 ounces) black beans, rinsed and drained
½	cup frozen corn kernels, cooked, drained, and cooled
½	red bell pepper, seeded and finely diced
½	green bell pepper, seeded and finely diced
½	red onion, finely diced
2	tablespoons finely chopped fresh cilantro leaves
1	tablespoon extra virgin olive oil
1	teaspoon red wine vinegar

• Heat a clean grill to medium high. Remove the chicken from the marinade, shaking off the excess, and season with salt and pepper. Discard the marinade. Grill until no longer pink in the middle, 6 to 8 minutes per side. Remove the chicken from the grill and let rest for 5 minutes.

• Divide the American Blend equally among individual plates. Drizzle with the dressing to taste. Top with a generous spoonful of the salsa, the sliced avocados, tortilla chips, and a chicken breast. Serve immediately.

¼	teaspoon cayenne pepper
	Kosher salt and freshly ground pepper

• Combine the black beans, corn, red bell pepper, green bell pepper, red onion, cilantro, oil, vinegar, and cayenne in a medium mixing bowl. Season with salt and pepper to taste. Toss to combine. Cover and refrigerate until ready to serve, up to 1 day in advance.

tip The Black Bean and Corn Salsa is such a versatile and tasty condiment. Serve as a dip with chips, serve it with fajitas, or bring it to a barbecue as a side dish.

chicken tostada salad
with salsa verde

This salad is not only tasty, but it can be a low-fat indulgence if you use reduced-fat sour cream.

MAKES 4 DINNER SALADS

4	8-inch round flour tortillas
¾	cup coarsely shredded pepper Jack cheese
1	bag (8 ounces) Shredded Lettuce
2	cups shredded cooked chicken
¼	cup fresh cilantro leaves, coarsely chopped
1	cup jarred green salsa
	Kosher salt and freshly ground pepper
1	large tomato, diced
¼	cup sour cream

• Preheat oven to 395°F. Place the tortillas on a baking sheet and evenly cover with the shredded cheese. Bake until the cheese is melted and the tortillas are crunchy, about 8 minutes. Remove from the oven and transfer to serving plates.

• In a large salad bowl, toss together the Shredded Lettuce, chicken, and cilantro. Add the salsa. Season with salt and pepper to taste. Spoon salad evenly over the warm tortillas. Garnish with the tomato and sour cream. Serve immediately.

tip   Made from tomatillos, salsa verde, or green salsa, typically has a naturally sweet tangy yet mild taste. Look for it in your grocery store next to other jarred salsas. Substitute your favorite jarred salsa if you prefer.

orange chicken over mixed greens
with citrus vinaigrette

Chicken á l'Orange—salad style! A classic pairing, this chicken and orange combination is great to serve for a large dinner party. **MAKES 4 DINNER SALADS**

salad ....

⅔	cup freshly squeezed orange juice
2	tablespoons honey
3	small garlic cloves, minced
1	tablespoon minced fresh thyme or
	1½ teaspoons dried thyme
2	teaspoons finely grated orange peel
4	skinless, boneless chicken breasts
	Kosher salt and freshly ground black pepper
1	bag (5 ounces) Spring Mix
3	oranges, peeled, sectioned, and seeded
1	shallot, thinly sliced crosswise into rings
1	orange bell pepper, seeded and cut into thin strips

• In a large bowl whisk together the orange juice, honey, garlic, thyme, and orange peel. Add the chicken breasts and turn to coat. Cover, refrigerate, and marinate the chicken for 1 to 4 hours.

• Heat a clean grill to medium high. Remove the chicken from the marinade, shaking off the excess. Discard the marinade. Season the marinated chicken with salt and pepper. Grill until no longer pink in the middle, 6 to 8 minutes per side. Remove the chicken from the grill and rest for 5 minutes.

• In a large salad bowl, toss together the Spring Mix, orange slices, shallot, and bell pepper. Add the vinaigrette to taste and gently toss. Divide the salad among individual plates. Top each with a grilled chicken breast. Serve immediately.

citrus vinaigrette ....

2	tablespoons extra virgin olive oil
1	tablespoon white wine vinegar
¼	cup freshly squeezed orange juice
1	small garlic clove, minced
	Kosher salt and freshly ground pepper

• In a small bowl whisk together the oil, vinegar, orange juice, and garlic until well combined. Season with salt and pepper to taste. **MAKES ABOUT ⅓ CUP**

tip The finely grated peel of a citrus fruit is called the zest. To grate the peel of a citrus fruit, use the fine grating holes on a traditional cheese grater or a hand-held rasp zester. Always zest the citrus fruit before peeling or slicing.

chicken paillard
topped with fresh greens

Paillard is the French cooking term for a piece of meat that has been pounded thin and cooked quickly. This dish of warm chicken and a fresh salad makes a tasty light meal. **MAKES 4 DINNER SALADS**

¼	cup Balsamic Grainy Mustard Vinaigrette (see page 229)
4	skinless, boneless chicken breasts
	Kosher salt and freshly ground pepper
2	tablespoons extra virgin olive oil
1	cup halved cherry tomatoes
1	bag (5 ounces) Spring Mix
¼	cup shredded Parmesan cheese

• Prepare the Balsamic Grainy Mustard Vinaigrette.

• Place a chicken breast in a large resealable heavy duty plastic bag. Using a mallet or rolling pin, flatten to about ¼-inch thick. Remove the chicken from the bag and season with salt and pepper. Repeat with the additional chicken breasts.

• In a large nonstick skillet over medium-high heat, warm the oil until a few water droplets sizzle. Carefully add the chicken to the skillet and cook until golden brown and no longer pink in the middle, about 4 minutes per side. Remove the chicken from the skillet and keep warm.

• Place the tomato halves in the same skillet used to cook the chicken. Cook over medium-high heat, stirring often, until slightly charred.

• In a large salad bowl, toss together the Spring Mix, tomatoes, and cheese. Add the vinaigrette to taste and gently toss.

• Place a chicken breast on each plate. Top with the salad. Serve immediately.

tip For a lower-fat version, substitute cooking spray for the olive oil and use a nonstick skillet when cooking the chicken.

chicken florentine salad

Florentine is a cooking term for when spinach is used in the recipe. This Italian-inspired spinach salad with orzo makes a light and delicious one-dish meal. **MAKES 4 DINNER SALADS**

salad . . . .

4	skinless, boneless chicken breasts, grilled, cooled, and thinly sliced against the grain
½	cup pine nuts, toasted
¼	cup sliced black olives (available in a can)
3	tablespoons capers, drained and rinsed
1	bag (6 ounces) Baby Spinach
1	cup cooked orzo, drained, rinsed, and cooled to room temperature

• In a large salad bowl, toss together the sliced chicken, pine nuts, black olives, capers, Baby Spinach, and orzo. Add the vinaigrette to taste and gently toss to coat. Serve immediately.

lemon-parmesan vinaigrette . . . .

2	tablespoons freshly squeezed lemon juice
1	teaspoon Dijon mustard
½	small garlic clove, mashed to a paste (see tip on page 230 for instructions) or minced
¼	cup extra virgin olive oil
1	tablespoon finely shredded Parmesan cheese
	Kosher salt and freshly ground pepper

• In a small bowl whisk together the lemon juice, mustard, and garlic. Slowly add the oil in a steady stream, whisking to emulsify. Stir in the cheese. Season with salt and pepper to taste.
MAKES ABOUT ⅓ CUP

tip Available in the pasta section of your local market, orzo is a pasta shaped like grains of rice. Cook as per package directions. If making ahead of time, drizzle with olive oil and toss to prevent sticking.

club salad
with honey mustard dressing

A takeoff on the traditional club sandwich, this salad is a classic favorite. This honey mustard dressing was a popular item at my restaurant, Cheffie's. My customers used it for everything from a salad dressing to a condiment for sandwiches to a dip for chicken fingers. MAKES 4 DINNER SALADS

salad ....

1	bag (11 ounces) Just Lettuce®
¼	cup coarsely shredded Monterey Jack cheese
¼	cup coarsely shredded Cheddar cheese
½	pound deli roast turkey, cut into strips
6	strips applewood smoked bacon, cooked, drained, and crumbled
1	large tomato, diced
¼	cup thinly sliced scallions

• Place the Just Lettuce in a large salad bowl. Add the dressing to taste and gently toss. Divide the salad among individual plates. Layer with the Jack cheese, Cheddar cheese, turkey, bacon, tomato, and scallions. Serve immediately.

honey mustard dressing ....

6	tablespoons mayonnaise
2	tablespoons Dijon mustard
2	tablespoons prepared yellow mustard
1½	tablespoons honey
2	to 3 tablespoons room temperature water
	Kosher salt and freshly ground pepper

• In a small bowl whisk together the mayonnaise, Dijon mustard, yellow mustard, and honey. Whisk in enough water to thin the mixture to desired consistency. Season with salt and pepper to taste. MAKES ABOUT ¾ CUP

tip Substitute any combination of your favorite deli meats in this salad.

CHAPTER THREE

meat

grilled steak salad
with marinated mushrooms, blue cheese crumbles, and red onion

Inspired by a traditional steak sandwich, this hearty main course salad will be sure to please.

MAKES 4 DINNER SALADS

salad . . . .

1	pound flank steak
	Kosher salt and freshly ground pepper
2	small garlic cloves, minced
1	bag (10 ounces) European Blend
2/3	cup drained marinated mushrooms, sliced
1	red onion, halved and thinly sliced
1/2	cup crumbled blue cheese (preferably Maytag)

• Heat a clean grill to medium high. Season the steak with salt and pepper to taste and the garlic. Grill, turning as needed, until medium rare, 4 to 6 minutes per side, or until desired doneness. Remove the steak from the grill and set aside to rest for 5 minutes before slicing.

• In a large salad bowl, toss the European Blend with the marinated mushrooms, red onion, and blue cheese. Add the vinaigrette to taste and gently toss. Season with salt and pepper to taste. Divide the salad among individual plates.

• Thinly slice the steak against the grain. Arrange the warm steak slices on top of the salad mixture. Serve immediately.

red wine dijon vinaigrette . . . .

2	tablespoons red wine vinegar
1	teaspoon Dijon Mustard
6	tablespoons extra-virgin olive oil
	Kosher salt and freshly ground pepper

• Combine the vinegar and mustard in a small bowl and whisk together. Slowly add the oil in a stream, whisking to emulsify. Season with salt and pepper to taste. MAKES ABOUT 1/4 CUP

tip This salad is a great use for leftover steak or roast beef.

blt salad

Bacon, lettuce, and tomato—the combination has a sandwich named after it, so why not a salad too?

MAKES 4 DINNER SALADS

¼	cup Buttermilk Ranch Dressing (see page 232)
1	bag (10 ounces) Lettuce Trio
4	Roma tomatoes, thinly sliced
½	red onion, halved and thinly sliced
½	pound applewood smoked bacon, cooked and drained on paper towels

• Prepare the Buttermilk Ranch Dressing.

• Divide the Lettuce Trio among individual plates.

• Generously drizzle with the dressing to taste. Top with the tomato slices, onion, and bacon strips.

tip Applewood smoked bacon is typically center-cut pork bacon that has been smoked over applewood chips. The result is a naturally sweet, smoky flavor.

taco salad

This salad is not for the diet conscious—but I guarantee you will enjoy every calorie. **Makes 4 dinner salads**

1	pound ground beef
1	package (1.25 ounces) taco seasoning
2	bags (8 ounces each) Shredded Lettuce
1	can (15 ounces) kidney beans or black beans, rinsed and drained
2	tomatoes, diced
2	ripe avocados, peeled and diced
1	small white onion, diced
1½	cups shredded sharp Cheddar cheese
2	cups tortilla chips
1½	cups salsa
1	cup sour cream
¼	cup pickled sliced jalapeños (optional)

• Brown the ground beef in a skillet over medium heat. Add the taco seasoning package and mix well. Set aside. (Place in a colander to drain excess fat, if desired.)

• Divide the Shredded Lettuce among individual bowls. Spoon a generous serving of the cooked beef in the center of each bed of lettuce. Add the beans, tomatoes, avocados, white onion, and cheese. Tuck the tortilla chips into the sides of the salad. Generously drizzle with the salsa to taste. Garnish with the sour cream and jalapeños, if desired. Serve immediately.

tip To make a lighter version, use lean ground beef or substitute ground turkey or chicken, omit the avocado, and use fat-free cheese and fat-free sour cream.

italian chef salad

In the United States, a chef salad is traditionally made using sliced deli meats and cheeses. This version gives it a European twist by substituting classic Italian deli items for the American staples. **MAKES 4 DINNER SALADS**

salad . . . .

1	bag (10 ounces) Italian Blend
¼	red onion, halved and thinly sliced
	Kosher salt and freshly ground pepper
2	Roma tomatoes, thinly sliced
8	thin slices Genoa salami, cut into strips
1	block (4 ounces) Parmesan cheese, shaved with a vegetable peeler
8	pepperoncinis

• In a large salad bowl, toss the Italian Blend and red onion together. Add the vinaigrette to taste and gently toss. Season with salt and pepper to taste. Divide the salad equally among the plates.

• Top the salad with the tomatoes, salami, and cheese. Garnish with the pepperoncinis. Serve immediately.

italian vinaigrette with fresh herbs . . . .

2	tablespoons red wine vinegar
1	shallot, minced
1	tablespoon freshly squeezed lemon juice
½	small garlic clove, mashed to a paste (see tip on page 230 for instructions) or minced
6	tablespoons extra-virgin olive oil
1	teaspoon coarsely chopped fresh oregano leaves
2	fresh basil leaves, coarsely chopped
	Kosher salt and freshly ground pepper

• In a small bowl whisk together the vinegar, shallot, lemon juice, and garlic. Slowly add the olive oil in a stream, whisking to emulsify. Stir in the oregano and basil. Season with salt and pepper to taste. MAKES ABOUT ¼ CUP

tip If making the vinaigrette in advance, chop and add the herbs just before serving. This helps keep the herbs vibrant green. If need be, dried herbs can be substituted for the fresh. Since dried herbs are more concentrated in flavor, use half the amount.

thai beef salad

Thanks to the mint and cilantro, this salad is refreshingly light. It's the perfect dish for a hot summer night.
MAKES 4 DINNER SALADS

salad ....

1	pound flank steak
	Kosher salt and freshly ground black pepper
½	cucumber, peeled, halved lengthwise, seeded, and thinly sliced
2	shallots, thinly sliced crosswise into rings
1	tablespoon coarsely chopped fresh cilantro
1	tablespoon coarsely chopped fresh mint
1	bag (10 ounces) Hearts of Romaine
½	cup coarsely chopped unsalted, roasted peanuts

• Place the steak in a shallow dish. Pour ⅓ of the dressing over the steak, turning to coat. Cover, refrigerate, and marinate 1 to 2 hours. Reserve the remaining dressing for use later.

• Heat a clean grill to medium high. Remove the steak from the marinade, shaking off excess. Discard the marinade. Season both sides of the steak with salt and pepper. Grill, turning as needed, until medium rare, 4 to 6 minutes per side, or until desired doneness. Remove the steak from the grill and set aside to rest for 5 to 10 minutes before slicing. Slice thinly against the grain.

• In a large bowl toss together the sliced steak, cucumber, shallots, cilantro, and mint. Add the remaining dressing to taste, reserving some to drizzle on top of the Hearts of Romaine, and gently toss.

• Divide the Hearts of Romaine equally among the plates and drizzle with the remaining dressing. Generously spoon the warm steak mixture over the beds of lettuce. Garnish with the chopped peanuts. Serve immediately.

dressing and marinade ....

¼	cup freshly squeezed lime juice
¼	cup fish sauce
2	teaspoons dark brown sugar
¼	teaspoon red pepper flakes

• In a small bowl whisk together the lime juice, fish sauce, brown sugar, and red pepper flakes until the sugar has dissolved. MAKES ABOUT ½ CUP

tip If you like more spice, substitute finely diced jalapeño or serrano chiles for the red pepper flakes in the dressing.

Known as "nam plah" in Thailand, fish sauce is an indispensable ingredient in Thai kitchens. Used to add saltiness to dishes, it is a condiment made from fermented anchovies, salt, and water. There is no perfect substitute for its unique flavor. A strong soy sauce would probably be the best option.

antipasti platter

Meaning "before the meal" in Italian, antipasti is the perfect appetizer for just about any party.

MAKES 8 APPETIZER SALADS

5	tablespoons extra-virgin olive oil, divided
1	tablespoon lemon zest
½	teaspoon red pepper flakes
4	small garlic cloves, peeled
1½	cups green Sicilian olives
1½	cups Kalamata olives
10	to 12 bocconcini (small fresh mozzarella balls), drained
3	fresh basil leaves, thinly sliced

	Kosher salt and freshly ground pepper
1	bag (5 ounces) Baby Arugula
1	pound assorted thinly sliced Italian deli meats, such as Genoa salami, spicy cappocollo, prosciutto, and mortadella
2	roasted red bell peppers (see page 176 for roasting instructions), thinly sliced (about 1 cup)
1	box (4 ounces) grissini (thin Italian breadsticks)

• In a medium bowl combine 3 tablespoons of the olive oil, lemon zest, red pepper flakes, garlic cloves, Sicilian olives, and Kalamata olives. Cover and marinate overnight in the refrigerator. Use within 2 days.

• In a small bowl toss the bocconcini with the remaining 2 tablespoons olive oil and the basil. Season with salt and pepper to taste.

• On a large platter arrange a bed of Baby Arugula. Arrange the deli meats, roasted red peppers, marinated olives, and bocconcini on top. Serve with the grissini on the side.

tip Jarred roasted red peppers save time, but I prefer the taste and texture of fresh roasted peppers for this dish where the peppers stand on their own.

grilled pork tenderloin salad
with apricot balsamic vinaigrette

I have to credit my dad and my step-mother for this sweet vinaigrette. Their concoction, invented to lessen the tart vinegar flavor of classic balsamic vinaigrette, is a wonderful match with grilled pork or poultry.
MAKES 4 DINNER SALADS

salad . . . .

½   cup apricot preserves
2   tablespoons white wine vinegar
1   tablespoon Dijon mustard
½   teaspoon ground ginger
1   to 1¼ pounds pork tenderloin
     Kosher salt and freshly ground pepper
1   bag (10 ounces) European Blend
½   cup drained and sliced canned or
     jarred apricot halves
½   cup dried cherries
¼   cup thinly sliced scallions
¼   cup sliced almonds, toasted

• Heat a clean grill to medium high.

• To prepare an apricot glaze whisk together the apricot preserves, vinegar, mustard, and ginger in a small bowl.

• Season the pork tenderloin with salt and pepper. Grill over medium-high heat until barely pink in the middle, brushing with the apricot glaze the last 2 minutes of cooking per side, 5 to 6 minutes per side.

• Remove the tenderloin from the heat and set aside to rest for 5 to 10 minutes before slicing. Slice thinly across the grain.

• In a large salad bowl, toss together the European Blend, apricots, cherries, scallions, and almonds.

• Add the vinaigrette to taste and gently toss. Divide equally among individual plates. Arrange the pork tenderloin slices on top of the salad. Serve immediately.

tip   When cooking pork, or any meat, it is best to use a meat thermometer as your guide for doneness. Pork is safely cooked through when an instant-read thermometer reaches 165°F when placed in the thickest part of the meat.

apricot balsamic vinaigrette . . . .

2　　tablespoons balsamic vinegar

½　　teaspoon yellow or Dijon mustard

　　　Dash of soy sauce

1　　garlic clove, minced

1　　teaspoon apricot preserves

¼　　cup extra-virgin olive oil

　　　Kosher salt and freshly ground pepper

• In a small bowl whisk together the vinegar, mustard, soy sauce, garlic, and apricot preserves.

• Slowly add the oil in a stream, whisking to emulsify. Season with salt and pepper to taste.

MAKES ABOUT ⅓ CUP

bbq pulled pork salad

All barbeque aficionados have heard of the "world famous" Rendezvous Restaurant in Memphis, Tennessee, owned by the Vergos family. My good friends Nick and Jenny Vergos developed this recipe using the Rendezvous' wet barbecue sauce, their tangy mustard slaw, and delicious Memphis-style pulled pork barbecue.

MAKES 4 DINNER SALADS

salad . . . .

2	cups Memphis Mustard Cole Slaw (see page 223)
4	cups pulled pork
1	cup barbecue sauce (I recommend one of the Memphis favorites: Rendezvous or Corky's)
1	bag (10 ounces) Hearts of Romaine
4	beefsteak tomatoes, quartered

• Prepare the Memphis Mustard Cole Slaw.

• In a large bowl toss together the pork and barbecue sauce.

• Divide the Hearts of Romaine among individual plates. Drizzle the dressing over the Hearts of Romaine to taste. Top with a one-fourth of the pork, a large spoonful of slaw, and the tomatoes.

bbq ranch dressing . . . .

1/2	cup Buttermilk Ranch Dressing (see page 232)
3	tablespoons barbecue sauce (I recommend one of the Memphis favorites: Rendezvous or Corky's)

• Prepare the Buttermilk Ranch Dressing. Add the barbecue sauce and whisk until well combined.

MAKES ABOUT 1/2 CUP

tip If you prefer, substitute chopped chicken for the pork.

prosciutto and melon salad

Reducing the balsamic vinegar makes a sweet and syrupy addition to this classic prosciutto and melon combination.
MAKES 6 APPETIZER SALADS

salad . . . .

1	melon (honeydew or cantaloupe), halved, and seeded
18	thin slices prosciutto
1	bag (7 ounces) Riviera™ Blend
2	tablespoons extra-virgin olive oil
	Kosher salt and freshly ground pepper

• Cut the melon into 18 wedges and remove the rind. Wrap each melon wedge with a slice of prosciutto.

• In a large salad bowl, toss the Riviera Blend with the oil and season with salt and pepper to taste.

• Divide the salad equally among individual plates. Arrange 3 wrapped melon wedges on each plate. Drizzle with the reduced balsamic vinegar. Serve immediately.

dressing . . . .

1	cup balsamic vinegar

• In a small saucepan bring the balsamic vinegar to a boil. Reduce the heat and simmer until syrupy and reduced by half. Remove from the heat and set aside to cool to room temperature. MAKES ABOUT ½ CUP

tip Prosciutto di Parma is a dry-cured ham from central and northern Italy. It can be freshly sliced at some deli counters, and many grocery stores now carry prepacked slices in their deli cases.

beef tenderloin with mâche

Traditionally paired with beef tenderloin, horseradish dressing gives this tenderloin salad a great kick.

MAKES 4 DINNER SALADS

salad . . . .

1½	pounds beef tenderloin, trimmed
	Kosher salt and freshly ground pepper
1	tablespoon olive oil
1	bag (3.5 ounces) Mâche Rosettes
½	cup thinly sliced chives

• Preheat oven to 375°F. Season the beef with salt and pepper. In an ovenproof skillet over high heat, warm the oil until a few water droplets sizzle in pan. Sear the beef until well browned on all sides, about 2 minutes per side. Transfer the pan to the oven and roast until medium rare, about 15 minutes, or until desired doneness. Remove from the oven and set aside to rest for 5 minutes. Slice the tenderloin into 4 pieces.

• To serve, arrange the sliced beef tenderloin on each individual plate. Top with the Mâche Rosettes. Drizzle with the dressing to taste. Garnish with the chives. Serve immediately.

horseradish dressing . . . .

¼	cup plain yogurt
2	tablespoons sour cream
1	tablespoon prepared white horseradish
2	tablespoons mayonnaise
	Kosher salt and freshly ground pepper

• In a small bowl whisk together the yogurt, sour cream, horseradish, and mayonnaise. Season with salt and pepper to taste. MAKES ABOUT ½ CUP

tip Mâche, also commonly called lamb's lettuce, has a delicate, slightly sweet flavor. Thanks to some innovative farmers in California, this traditionally French ingredient is starting to pop up in grocery stores across the United States.

grilled lamb and tabbouleh salad

The grilled onions and tabbouleh give this Middle Eastern-inspired salad a delicious complexity.

MAKES 4 DINNER SALADS

salad . . . .

1	pound trimmed boneless leg of lamb
	Kosher salt and freshly ground pepper
1	red onion, sliced into rings
2	tablespoons extra-virgin olive oil
1	bag (6 ounces) Baby Spinach
1	cup prepared tabbouleh
½	cup crumbled feta cheese

• Preheat a clean grill to medium high.

• Butterfly the lamb by cutting horizontally through the thickest part of the meat, leaving about 1 inch still attached. (The goal is to have a piece of meat that is of even thickness.) Open flat and season with salt and pepper.

• Place the sliced onion in a medium bowl and drizzle with the oil; toss to coat.

• Place the lamb and onion slices on the prepared grill. Grill the lamb until medium rare, about 8 minutes per side, or until desired doneness. Grill the onion slices in a grilling basket until tender, about 5 minutes per side.

• Set the lamb aside to rest for 5 to 10 minutes before slicing. Thinly slice the lamb diagonally across the grain.

• Place the Baby Spinach in a large salad bowl. Add the dressing to taste and gently toss. Divide the salad among individual plates. Spoon about ¼ cup of the tabbouleh over the top. Arrange the lamb slices and onions over each salad. Garnish with the crumbled feta cheese. Serve immediately.

vinaigrette . . . .

2	tablespoons red wine vinegar
1	tablespoon freshly squeezed lemon juice
6	tablespoons extra-virgin olive oil
	Kosher salt and freshly ground pepper

• In a small bowl whisk together the vinegar and lemon juice. Slowly add the oil in a stream, whisking to emulsify. Season with salt and pepper to taste.

MAKES ABOUT ¼ CUP

tip If you can't find premade tabbouleh at your local market deli or in the prepackaged deli cases, make your own. Just prepare a box of tabbouleh wheat (usually in the rice section) as per the package directions and add chopped tomatoes, cucumber, and parsley. Season with salt and pepper to taste.

fajita salad

Shake-up some margaritas to accompany this sizzling salad in homemade tortilla bowls. Add some hot sauce to spice it up a bit if you like. **MAKES 4 DINNER SALADS**

salad . . . .

2	tablespoons freshly squeezed lime juice
3	tablespoons tequila
1	tablespoon ground cumin
1	garlic clove, minced
1½	pounds flank steak, cut across the grain into ½-inch thick slices
4	8-inch round flour tortillas
	Kosher salt and freshly ground pepper
1	tablespoon olive oil
1	red bell pepper, seeded and thinly sliced
1	green bell pepper, seeded and thinly sliced
½	red onion, halved and thinly sliced
1	bag (10 ounces) Leafy Romaine

• In a small bowl whisk together the lime juice, tequila, cumin, and garlic. Pour the marinade over the flank steak, cover, and marinate 1 hour.

• Preheat the oven to 375°F. In ovenproof bowls similar in size to your serving dish, place the tortillas. Press down on each tortilla until it is the shape of a bowl. Bake until slightly golden and crispy, about 10 minutes. Remove from the oven and let cool to room temperature.

• Remove the steak from the marinade, shaking off the excess. Discard the marinade. Season with salt and pepper.

• In a grill pan over high heat, warm the oil until a few water droplets sizzle in the pan. Add the steak and sear, stirring often, until well browned, 3 to 4 minutes. Add the red bell pepper, green bell pepper, and onion and cook, stirring often, until the vegetables are browned and the steak is cooked to desired doneness, about 4 more minutes for medium rare.

• Place the Leafy Romaine in a large salad bowl. Add the vinaigrette to taste and gently toss. Season with salt and pepper to taste.

• Place the tortilla "bowls" on individual dishes. Fill with the Leafy Romaine. Top with the warm fajita mixture. Garnish with the Pico de Gallo. Serve immediately.

tip   If feeding a crowd, serve this salad true "fajita-style": on a platter with warm tortillas on the side.

pico de gallo . . . .

½   small white onion, finely diced

1   large tomato, seeded and diced

½   green bell pepper, seeded and finely diced

1   teaspoon chopped seeded fresh jalapeño

3   tablespoons freshly squeezed lime juice

1   tablespoon extra-virgin olive oil

   Kosher salt and freshly ground pepper

• In a medium bowl toss together the onion, tomato, bell pepper, jalapeño, lime juice, and oil. Season with salt and pepper to taste.

lime vinaigrette . . . .

4   tablespoons freshly squeezed lime juice

2   tablespoons freshly squeezed orange juice

1   tablespoon sugar

2   tablespoons canola oil

   Kosher salt and freshly ground pepper

• In a small bowl whisk together the lime juice, orange juice, and sugar until the sugar has dissolved. Slowly add the oil in a stream, whisking to emulsify. Season to taste with salt and pepper. MAKES ABOUT ¼ CUP

seafood

seared salmon over mixed greens
with dried cranberries, feta cheese, and candied pecans

I just love the different flavors in this salad. **MAKES 4 DINNER SALADS**

salad . . . .

4	boneless salmon fillets (4 to 6 ounces each)
	Kosher salt and freshly ground pepper
2	tablespoons extra-virgin olive oil
1	bag (5 ounces) Spring Mix
½	cup dried cranberries
¼	cup thinly sliced scallions
½	cup crumbled feta cheese

• Season the salmon with salt and pepper. In a large skillet over medium heat, warm the oil until a few water droplets sizzle in pan. Sear the salmon, skin side up, until the meat is well browned and easily releases from the pan, 4 to 6 minutes. Turn and cook until the fish is medium rare, about 5 more minutes, or until desired doneness.

• While the salmon is cooking, toss the Spring Mix with the cranberries, scallions, feta cheese, and ¾ cup pecans in a large salad bowl. Reserve the remaining pecans for another use. Add the vinaigrette to taste, reserving some to drizzle on top of fish, and gently toss. Season with salt and pepper to taste. Divide the salad among individual plates.

• Place the salmon fillets on top of the salad mixture. Drizzle the salmon with the reserved vinaigrette. Serve immediately.

candied pecans . . . .

1	large egg white
1	teaspoon salt
⅓	cup sugar
1	teaspoon Worcestershire sauce
1	tablespoon paprika
3	tablespoons unsalted butter, melted and cooled to room temperature
1	teaspoon cayenne pepper
2	cups pecan halves

• Preheat the oven to 375°F.

• In a large bowl whisk the egg white and salt until the mixture is frothy. Add the sugar, Worcestershire

tip This salad is also great with grilled chicken.

sauce, paprika, cayenne pepper, and butter. Whisk until well combined. Gently stir in the pecans.

• Spread the pecans on a nonstick rimmed baking pan in a single layer. Bake for 30 minutes, stirring after the first 15 minutes to prevent sticking. Remove from the oven and cool to room temperature. Pecans can be stored up to two days in an airtight container.

raspberry vinaigrette . . . .

3   tablespoons raspberry balsamic vinegar
1   tablespoon freshly squeezed lemon juice
5   tablespoons canola oil
      Kosher salt and freshly ground pepper

• In a small bowl whisk together the vinegar and lemon juice. Slowly add the oil in a steady stream, whisking until emulsified. Season with salt and pepper to taste. MAKES ABOUT $1/4$ CUP

tuna niçoise

This yummy tossed version of the French classic goes great with a crusty piece of French bread or tucked into pita bread for an out-of-the-ordinary tuna sandwich. MAKES 4 DINNER SALADS

½ cup Lemon Vinaigrette (see page 231)

8 small red new potatoes

¼ pound haricots verts or fresh green beans, trimmed

1 bag (10 ounces) Leafy Romaine

1 can (6 ounces) tuna, drained and flaked

2 radishes, trimmed and thinly sliced

½ cup Niçoise olives, pitted

¼ cup capers, drained and rinsed

½ red onion, halved and thinly sliced

• Prepare the Lemon Vinaigrette.

• Place the potatoes in a large pot of salted water and bring to a boil over high heat. Reduce the heat to medium low and simmer until the potatoes are fork tender, 10 to 15 minutes. Drain in a colander and rinse under cold water to cool. When cool enough to comfortably handle, cut the potatoes into fourths

• While the potatoes are cooking, bring another large pot of salted water to a boil over high heat. Add the haricots verts and cook until just tender, 3 to 4 minutes. Drain in a colander and rinse with cold water until cooled.

• In a large salad bowl, combine the Leafy Romaine, potatoes, haricots verts, tuna, radishes, olives, capers, and red onion. Add the vinaigrette to taste and toss until well combined. Serve immediately.

tip Haricots verts are tender, skinny French green beans. Many grocery stores now carry them in either the fresh or the frozen vegetable section. If you can't find them, just use traditional fresh green beans. To save some time you can cook the potatoes and haricots verts ahead. Cool and refrigerate until ready to toss all the ingredients.

salmon and asparagus salad
with pesto vinaigrette

Pesto can be used to garnish so much more than pasta. Use it as a condiment for grilled fish or even as the base of a salad dressing as in this recipe. Making pesto from scratch is a breeze if you have fresh basil. If fresh basil is not available, feel free to use store-bought pesto. Just mix 2 tablespoons of the pesto with 1 tablespoon red wine vinegar and 2 tablespoons extra-virgin olive oil. **MAKES 4 DINNER SALADS**

salad . . . .

4	boneless salmon fillets (4 to 6 ounces each)
	Kosher salt and freshly ground pepper
1	tablespoon olive oil
½	bunch (about ½ pound) asparagus spears, trimmed
1	bag (10 ounces) Hearts of Romaine
¾	cup cherry tomatoes, halved

• Preheat oven to 400°F. Place the salmon fillets, skin side down, in a shallow baking dish. Season with salt and pepper to taste. Drizzle with the olive oil. Bake until just cooked through and easily flakes to the touch, about 15 minutes. Remove from the oven and let cool to room temperature. Once the salmon has cooled, gently flake with a fork, discarding the skin.

• Cut the trimmed asparagus spears into 1½-inch pieces. In a medium pot bring salted water to a boil. Add the asparagus and cook until vibrant green and crisp tender, 1 to 1½ minutes. Drain the asparagus and immerse in an ice water bath to stop the cooking process. Drain again and place in a large salad bowl. Add the Hearts of Romaine, salmon, and cherry tomatoes. Add the vinaigrette to taste and gently toss. Serve immediately.

pesto vinaigrette . . . .

¾	cup loosely packed fresh basil leaves, rinsed and patted dry
1	small garlic clove, minced
1	tablespoon finely grated Parmesan cheese
1	tablespoon pine nuts, toasted and cooled to room temperature
1½	tablespoons red wine vinegar
½	cup extra-virgin olive oil
	Kosher salt and freshly ground pepper

• In a food processor or blender, pureé the basil, garlic, Parmesan cheese, pine nuts, vinegar, and oil until smooth. Season with salt and pepper to taste. MAKES ABOUT ¾ CUP tip To toast pine nuts, spread the nuts evenly on a baking sheet and place in a preheated 325°F oven. Toast, stirring occasionally so that they evenly brown, until they start to turn golden and are fragrant, about 3 minutes. Remove from the oven and let cool. Pine nuts can also be toasted in your toaster oven.

butter lettuce
tossed with smoked salmon, capers, and dill

A delicate lemon vinaigrette ties together the classic pairings of smoked salmon with dill and capers in this light salad. **MAKES 4 DINNER OR 6 APPETIZER SALADS**

¼	cup Lemon Vinaigrette (see page 231)
1	bag (7 ounces) Riviera™ Blend
6	ounces sliced smoked salmon, cut into strips
¼	cup capers, drained and rinsed
¼	red onion, halved and thinly sliced
2	tablespoons coarsely chopped fresh dill

• Prepare the Lemon Vinaigrette.

• In a large bowl toss together the Riviera Blend, smoked salmon, capers, red onion, and dill. Add the vinaigrette to taste and gently toss. Serve immediately.

seared tuna salad
with honey-lime cilantro dressing

The tropical flavors of the lime and cilantro dressing, as well as the fresh mango, are wonderful complements to seared sushi-grade fresh tuna. MAKES 4 DINNER SALADS

salad . . . .

4	sushi-grade tuna steaks (4 to 6 ounces each)
	Kosher salt and freshly ground pepper
2	tablespoons extra-virgin olive oil
1	bag (5 ounces) Spring Mix
1	mango, pitted, diced, and peeled
½	red onion, halved and thinly sliced
¼	cup pickled ginger (optional)

• Season the tuna with salt and pepper. In a large skillet over medium-high heat, warm the oil until a few water droplets sizzle in the pan. Quickly sear the tuna, leaving the tuna rare inside, until well browned and easily releases from pan, about 2 minutes per side. Transfer to a cutting board and slice thinly.

• In a large salad bowl, toss the Spring Mix with the mango and red onion. Add the dressing to taste, reserving some to drizzle on top of the fish, and gently toss. Season with salt and pepper to taste.

• Divide the salad equally among individual plates. Place the sliced tuna next to the salad. Drizzle the reserved dressing over the tuna. Garnish with the pickled ginger, if desired. Serve immediately.

honey-lime cilantro dressing . . . .

⅓	cup freshly squeezed lime juice
1	tablespoon freshly squeezed lemon juice
2	tablespoons honey
3	tablespoons extra-virgin olive oil
3	tablespoons coarsely chopped fresh cilantro leaves
	Kosher salt and freshly ground pepper

• In a small bowl whisk together the lime juice, lemon juice, honey, and oil until well combined. Stir in the cilantro. Season with salt and pepper to taste. MAKES ABOUT ½ CUP

tip To cut a mango, first slice the fruit lengthwise along its center seed to get two halves. Remove the seed. Then place the mango halves skin side down on a cutting board. Using a paring knife, create a crosshatch pattern through the meat, but not going through the skin. Finally, flip the mango halves inside out and slice off the squares of fruit.

pancetta-wrapped scallops
with rosemary-lemon vinaigrette

If you want to impress your guests, this is the salad. It looks and tastes fabulous—and yet is easy to prepare. Pancetta is Italian bacon. If you cannot find it in your deli or in the refrigerated deli meat section at your grocery, simply substitute bacon strips. Make note, however, that depending on the thickness of the bacon, it may take longer for the bacon to crisp. **MAKES 4 DINNER SALADS OR 6 APPETIZER SALADS**

salad . . . .

12	large sea scallops
½	pound pancetta, thinly sliced (at least 12 slices)
1	bag (5 ounces) Spring Mix
	Kosher salt and freshly ground pepper

• Rinse the scallops, pat dry, and place in a large bowl. Pour half the vinaigrette over the scallops; toss to coat. Reserve the remaining vinaigrette for the salad. Cover, refrigerate, and let the scallops marinate for 1 hour.

• Preheat the oven to 375°F. Remove the scallops from the marinade and wrap each scallop with one slice of pancetta. Place the scallops 1-inch apart on an ungreased rimmed baking pan.

• Bake until the pancetta is crispy, about 10 minutes.

• Place the Spring Mix in a large salad bowl. Add the reserved vinaigrette to taste and gently toss. Season with salt and pepper to taste. Divide the salad equally among the plates. Arrange the scallops, equally divided, on the plates. Serve immediately.

rosemary-lemon vinaigrette . . . .

1	teaspoon finely grated lemon zest
¼	cup freshly squeezed lemon juice
½	cup extra-virgin olive oil
4	tablespoons minced fresh rosemary

• In a small bowl whisk together the lemon zest and lemon juice. Slowly add the oil in a steady stream, whisking to emulsify. Stir in the rosemary.
MAKES ABOUT ¾ CUP

tip Toothpicks can be used to secure the pancetta to the scallop if necessary. Just remember to remove them before serving. For easy cleanup, line your baking sheet with aluminum foil.

shrimp tossed with herb salad
and lemony ginger vinaigrette

With the abundance of fresh herbs and the lemony vinaigrette, this salad just sings of springtime. If you can't find the Fresh Herb Salad in your market, just add a mixture of fresh herbs, such as cilantro and dill, to your Spring Mix. MAKES 4 DINNER OR 6 APPETIZER SALADS

salad ....

1	tablespoon salt
1	lemon, cut into quarters
1	pound medium shrimp, peeled, tails removed, and deveined
1	bag (5 ounces) Fresh Herb Blend
1	carrot, peeled and shaved into wide ribbons with a vegetable peeler
1	red bell pepper, seeded and cut in thin strips
6	fresh chives, cut into ¼-inch pieces

• Fill a large pot with water and add the salt and lemon quarters. Bring to a boil. Add the shrimp and cook until opaque throughout, 3 to 5 minutes. Be careful not to over cook. Drain the shrimp and cool to room temperature. Discard the lemon quarters.

• In large salad bowl toss the Fresh Herb Blend, carrot, bell pepper, chives, and shrimp. Add the vinaigrette to taste and gently toss. Serve immediately.

lemony ginger vinaigrette ....

2	tablespoons white wine vinegar
1	teaspoon finely grated lemon zest
2	tablespoons fresh lemon juice
¼	teaspoon grated fresh peeled ginger
1	tablespoon sugar
6	tablespoons canola oil
	Kosher salt and freshly ground pepper

• In a small bowl whisk together the vinegar, lemon zest, lemon juice, ginger, sugar, and canola oil until the sugar has dissolved. Season with salt and pepper to taste. MAKES ABOUT ½ CUP

tip To save time, substitute peeled, cooked shrimp from your grocery store's seafood department.

shrimp stir-fry salad

I just love the fresh and spicy flavors of Thai cuisine. The cilantro and lemongrass are the perfect foils for the spicy chili pepper. MAKES 4 DINNER SALADS

salad . . . .

1	tablespoon peanut oil (or canola oil if allergic)
1	tablespoon red Thai curry paste
1	pound medium shrimp, peeled, tailes removed, deveined, and halved lengthwise
12	cherry tomatoes, halved
¼	cup scallions, sliced ½-inch long on the diagonal
1	bag (11.4 ounces) Asian Salad Blend

• In a wok over medium-high heat, warm the oil and curry paste, stirring often, until fragrant. Add the shrimp and cook, stirring occasionally, until opaque throughout, about 3 minutes. Transfer to a large bowl and set aside to cool.

• Add the tomatoes and the scallions to the shrimp. Add half the dressing to taste and gently toss.

• Place the Asian Salad Blend in a large salad bowl. Add the remaining dressing to taste and gently toss.

• Divide the Asian Salad Blend among the plates. Generously spoon the shrimp mixture on top. Serve immediately.

thai dressing . . . .

2	tablespoons dark brown sugar
1	teaspoon finely grated lime zest
¼	cup freshly squeezed lime juice
1	Thai chili pepper or Serrano pepper, seeded (if desired) and minced
2	stalks lemongrass, outer leaves removed and very thinly sliced
1	shallot, halved and thinly sliced
3	tablespoons finely chopped fresh cilantro

• In a small bowl whisk together the brown sugar, lime zest, and lime juice until the sugar is dissolved. Stir in the chili pepper, lemongrass, shallot, and cilantro. MAKES ABOUT ⅓ CUP

> tip Lemongrass is a perennial herb that, until recently, was grown mostly in Southeast Asia. It offers a light and refreshing lemony flavor. Thanks to the growing popularity of Thai food, it is now available in many supermarkets. If you can't find it, substitute 1 tablespoon of freshly squeezed lemon juice.

lobster salad
with grapefruit vinaigrette

Lobster salad may sound difficult . . . , but if your local grocer cooks the meat for you, this salad is a cinch to prepare. **Makes 4 dinner or 6 appetizer salads**

salad . . . .

2	1-pound lobsters, freshly cooked and shelled
¼	cup thinly sliced celery
½	red bell pepper, seeded and diced
1	tablespoon minced fresh basil
1	tablespoon minced fresh mint
1	bag (7 ounces) Riviera™ Blend, torn into small pieces

• Cut the lobster meat into ½-inch pieces. Place the lobster meat in a large salad bowl. Add the celery, red bell pepper, basil, mint, and the Riviera Blend. Add the vinaigrette to taste and gently toss. Serve immediately.

grapefruit vinaigrette . . . .

4	tablespoons freshly squeezed grapefruit juice
2	tablespoons freshly squeezed lime juice
1	tablespoon minced shallot
2	tablespoons canola oil
	Kosher salt and freshly ground pepper

• In a small bowl whisk together the grapefruit juice, lime juice, shallot, and oil until well combined. Season with salt and pepper to taste. **Makes about ⅓ cup**

tip To save time and mess, I recommend having your local grocery seafood department steam or boil the lobster for you. If you prefer to cook them yourself, simply drop the 1-pound lobsters in a large pot of boiling salted water, let the water return to a full boil, and then cook for ten minutes.

crawfish salad
with spicy cajun remoulade

Crawfish gives a classic Louisiana shrimp remoulade a spicy twist. Harvested in Southern coastal states such as Louisiana and Mississippi, crawfish are fresh water crustaceans similar to small lobsters. Ask your grocer's seafood manager to order it for you, fresh or frozen, in advance. MAKES 4 DINNER OR 6 APPETIZER SALADS

salad . . . .

1	pound cooked crawfish tails, fresh or frozen (if frozen, thaw overnight in the refrigerator and rinse before using)
¼	cup thinly sliced celery
½	small white onion, minced
1	bag (8 ounces) Triple Hearts™

• In a large salad bowl, toss together the crawfish meat, celery, and onion. Add the remoulade sauce to taste and gently toss.

• Divide the Triple Hearts equally among the plates. Generously top with a spoonful of the crawfish salad. Serve immediately.

spicy cajun remoulade . . . .

½	cup tarragon vinegar
2	tablespoons freshly squeezed lemon juice
¼	cup prepared white horseradish
¼	cup Creole (or spicy brown) mustard
2	tablespoons ketchup
1	small garlic clove, minced
1	teaspoon paprika
	Dash cayenne pepper
1	cup vegetable oil
	Kosher salt and freshly ground pepper

• In a blender combine the tarragon vinegar, lemon juice, horseradish, mustard, ketchup, garlic, paprika, cayenne, and vegetable oil. Season with salt and pepper to taste. MAKES ABOUT 2 CUPS

tip If tarragon vinegar is not available, make your own. In a small saucepan over medium heat, gently warm ¾ cup white wine vinegar and 1 tablespoon dried tarragon until tarragon is fragrant, about 3 minutes. Set aside until cooled completely and then strain.

spanish shrimp, orange, and olive salad

Oranges, olives, sherry, and shellfish are popular ingredients throughout Spain. This quick and easy salad gives you a taste of some of this country's extraordinary flavors. **MAKES 4 DINNER OR 6 APPETIZER SALADS**

salad . . . .

¾	pound medium shrimp, peeled, tails removed, and deveined
	Kosher salt and freshly ground pepper
2	tablespoons olive oil
1	small garlic clove, minced
3	oranges, peeled and thinly sliced
½	cup sliced Spanish green olives
1	teaspoon finely grated orange peel
1	bag (5 ounces) Baby Arugula

• Season the shrimp with salt and pepper. In a large skillet over medium-high heat, warm the oil until a few droplets of water sizzle in pan. Add the garlic and shrimp and cook, stirring occasionally, until the shrimp are opaque in the center, 3 to 5 minutes. Set aside and cool to room temperature.

• In a large bowl, toss together the shrimp, orange slices, olives, orange peel, and Baby Arugula. Add the sherry vinaigrette to taste and gently toss. Serve immediately.

sherry vinaigrette . . . .

1	shallot, minced
1	teaspoon Dijon mustard
2	tablespoons sherry wine vinegar
6	tablespoons extra-virgin olive oil
	Kosher salt and freshly ground pepper

• In a small bowl whisk together the shallot, mustard, and vinegar. Slowly add the olive oil in a stream, whisking to emulsify. Season with salt and pepper to taste. MAKES ABOUT ¼ CUP

tip Using store-bought cooked shrimp will save time, but cooking raw shrimp infuses the dish with a sweet garlic flavor.

maryland crab cake salad
with caper remoulade

I like to be able to savor the crab in my crab cakes rather than taste a lot of spices or breading. This recipe uses just enough filling to bind the crabmeat, letting the delicate lump crabmeat take center stage.

Makes 4 dinner or 8 appetizer salads

salad . . . .

1	pound jumbo lump crabmeat
1	egg, cracked into a small bowl
1	tablespoon mayonnaise
1	teaspoon Dijon mustard
1	teaspoon Worcestershire sauce
2	tablespoons minced fresh parsley
	Kosher salt and freshly ground pepper
½	red bell pepper, seeded and finely diced
1	shallot, minced
3	tablespoons breadcrumbs
¼	cup White Balsamic Vinaigrette (see page 7)
	Vegetable oil for frying
1	bag (8 ounces) Mediterranean Blend

• Pick through the crabmeat to remove any extra shell.

• In a medium bowl whisk together the egg, mayonnaise, mustard, Worcestershire sauce, and parsley. Season to taste with salt and pepper.

• Gently fold the crabmeat, red bell pepper, shallot, and breadcrumbs into the egg mixture. Shape into 8 crab cakes. Cover with plastic wrap and refrigerate for 30 minutes.

• Prepare the White Balsamic Vinaigrette.

• Fill a large skillet with vegetable oil about ¼-inch deep. Heat the oil over medium-high heat until a few droplets of water sizzle in pan. Fry the cakes until golden brown, about 5 minutes per side. Remove from the skillet and set aside; keep warm.

• Divide the Mediterranean Blend among individual plates. Drizzle the dressing over the salad to taste. Arrange the crab cakes on the salad. Garnish with a generous spoonful of caper remoulade. Serve immediately.

caper remoulade ....

¼ cup mayonnaise

¼ cup sour cream

2 tablespoons freshly squeezed lemon juice

4 tablespoons capers, drained and rinsed

   Kosher salt and freshly ground pepper

• In a small bowl whisk together the mayonnaise, sour cream, and lemon juice. Stir in the capers. Season with salt and pepper to taste. MAKES ABOUT ½ CUP

vegetables

warm fingerling potato salad
with bacon and croutons

A meal in itself, the flavor of the tender fingerling potatoes tossed with a fragrant garlic vinaigrette transports me to the French countryside. MAKES 4 DINNER OR 6 APPETIZER SALADS

¼	cup Garlic Vinaigrette (see page 230)
1	pound small fingerling potatoes, cleaned
3	tablespoons extra-virgin olive oil
½	thin baguette (8 ounces), thinly sliced
8	slices of bacon
1	bag (8 ounces) Field Greens

• Prepare the Garlic Vinaigrette.

• Fill a large pot with salted water. Add the potatoes and bring to a boil. Reduce the heat and simmer until the potatoes are fork tender, 8 to10 minutes. Drain and keep warm.

• In a large skillet over medium heat, warm the oil until a few water droplets sizzle in the pan. Cook the bread slices, stirring often, until golden brown and crisp, about 4 minutes. Using a slotted spoon transfer the croutons to a paper towel–lined plate to drain. In the same pan, cook the bacon, turning as needed, until crisp, 3 to 4 minutes. Transfer the bacon to a paper towel–lined plate to drain; keep warm.

• Place the warm potatoes in a large salad bowl and add the vinaigrette to taste. Toss to coat well. Add the Field Greens and toss gently. Tear the bacon into 1-inch pieces and add to the salad along with the croutons. Serve immediately.

tip Fingerlings are narrow finger-shaped heirloom potatoes. A longtime secret of restaurant chefs, these tender potatoes have a rich and buttery flavor unlike any other potato variety. Yukon Gold potatoes or red new potatoes are good substitutes.

greek salad

A traditional Greek salad chock-full of chopped tomatoes, cucumbers, Kalamata olives, and Feta cheese.
MAKES 4 DINNER OR 6 APPETIZER SALADS

salad . . . .

1	bag (8 ounces) Mediterranean Blend
2	Roma tomatoes, diced
½	red onion, halved and thinly sliced
½	green bell pepper, seeded and cut into thin strips
½	red bell pepper, seeded and cut into thin strips
1	small cucumber, halved lengthwise and thinly sliced
¼	cup thinly sliced scallions
½	cup Kalamata olives, pitted
⅓	cup crumbled Feta cheese

• In a large salad bowl, toss together the Mediterranean Blend, tomatoes, red onion, green and red bell peppers, cucumber, and scallions. Add the dressing to taste and gently toss. Sprinkle the olives and Feta cheese over the salad. Serve immediately.

greek vinaigrette . . . .

3	tablespoons red wine vinegar
1	teaspoon freshly squeezed lemon juice
1	teaspoon dried oregano
1	small garlic clove, mashed to a paste (see page 230 for instructions) or minced
6	tablespoons extra-virgin olive oil
	Kosher salt and freshly ground pepper

• In a small bowl whisk together the vinegar, lemon juice, oregano, and garlic. Slowly add the oil in a steady stream, whisking until emulsified. Season to taste with salt and pepper. MAKES ABOUT ⅓ CUP

tip Garnish with toasted pita wedges, pita strips, or your favorite pita chips.

asparagus, roasted red pepper, and arugula salad

This tasty salad makes an elegant presentation for a dinner party first course. Arrange on a platter for a wonderful buffet offering. MAKES 4 APPETIZER SALADS

salad . . . .

1	bunch (about 1 pound) asparagus, trimmed
1	bag (5 ounces) Baby Arugula
1	roasted red bell pepper (see page 176 for roasting instructions), thinly sliced (about ½ cup)
⅓	cup Kalamata olives, pitted and finely chopped
½	small red onion, finely chopped

• Bring a medium pot of salted water to a boil. Add the asparagus and cook until vibrant green and crisp tender, 1 to 1½ minutes. Drain the asparagus and immerse in an ice water bath to stop the cooking process. Drain again and set aside.

• On each plate, place a bed of Baby Arugula. Layer the asparagus on top. Arrange the roasted pepper on top of the asparagus. Generously drizzle with the vinaigrette to taste. Garnish with the olives and red onion.

white balsamic and grainy mustard vinaigrette . . . .

2	tablespoons white balsamic vinegar
1	tablespoon whole-grain Dijon mustard
6	tablespoons extra-virgin olive oil
	Kosher salt and freshly ground pepper

• In a small bowl whisk together the vinegar and mustard. Slowly add the oil in a steady stream, whisking to emulsify. Season with salt and pepper to taste. MAKES ABOUT ¼ CUP

tip The coarse seeds in whole-grain mustard add texture and a depth of flavor to traditional Dijon mustard. Despite being similar in appearance, the French-style whole-grain mustard has a more delicate flavor than spicy Creole mustard. Dijon mustard is the proper substitute.

layered chop salad

What a presentation! This layered salad is a great idea for a buffet dinner party. MAKES **10** SIDE SALADS

1¼	cups Buttermilk Garlic Dressing (see page 39)
1	bag (16 ounces) frozen green peas, thawed
1	can (15 ounces) chickpeas, rinsed and drained
1	package (8 ounces) Shredded Lettuce
2	red bell peppers, seeded and diced
1	bunch scallions, thinly sliced
1	bag (10 ounces) Shredded Carrots
4	cucumbers, halved lengthwise, seeded, and diced
4	Roma tomatoes, quartered lengthwise, seeded, and diced
1	can (6 ounces) fried onions

• Prepare the Buttermilk Garlic Dressing.

• In a large glass bowl layer the green peas, chickpeas, Shredded Lettuce, red bell peppers, scallions, carrots, cucumbers, and tomatoes. Pour the dressing over the top and set aside until the layers are soaked through, about 5 minutes. Just before serving, top with the fried onions.

tip This salad can be prepared a few hours in advance up until the point where you add the dressing.

caprese salad

The Italian word Caprese refers to a simple, yet sublime, salad made using ripe summer tomatoes, fresh mozzarella, and basil fresh from the garden. **MAKES 6 APPETIZER OR SIDE SALADS**

salad . . . .

1	bag (5 ounces) Spring Mix
4	to 5 medium tomatoes, sliced crosswise (18 slices)
1	pound fresh mozzarella (approximately 2 balls), sliced into rounds (18 slices)
18	large fresh basil leaves or 36 small leaves
	Kosher salt and freshly ground pepper

• Place the Spring Mix in a large salad bowl. Add the vinaigrette to taste and gently toss. Divide the salad among the plates.

• In three layers per salad, arrange the tomatoes, mozzarella, and basil leaves. Season with salt and pepper to taste. Serve immediately.

balsamic vinaigrette . . . .

2	tablespoons balsamic vinegar
6	tablespoons extra-virgin olive oil
	Kosher salt and freshly ground pepper

• Place the vinegar in a small bowl. Slowly add the oil in a steady stream, whisking to emulsify. Season with salt and pepper to taste. **MAKES ABOUT ¼ CUP**

> tip This salad should only be made with fresh, moist mozzarella; never the smoked yellow variety. The best mozzarella is made from buffalo milk, but it is expensive and can be hard to find. Fresh mozzarella made from cow's milk is more affordable and has the same creamy texture as buffalo.

summer vegetable salad

All year long I dream of the few short weeks every summer when my father-in-law's vegetable garden yields its tender, delicious vegetables. This salad highlights some of my favorite summer produce.

MAKES 6 APPETIZER OR SIDE SALADS

1½	cups Champagne Vinaigrette (see page 27)
1	bag (5 ounces) Fresh Herb Blend
½	red onion, halved and thinly sliced
2	patty pan squash, sliced lengthwise and cut into thin matchsticks
2	baby zucchini, sliced lengthwise and cut into thin matchsticks
½	cup cherry tomatoes, halved
1	red bell pepper, seeded and thinly sliced
4	radishes, trimmed and thinly sliced into rounds
½	cup shredded aged Monterey Jack cheese

• Prepare the Champagne Vinaigrette dressing.

• In a large salad bowl, toss together the Fresh Herb Blend, onion, squash, zucchini, tomatoes, red bell pepper, and radishes. Add the vinaigrette to taste and toss gently. Garnish with the Monterey Jack cheese. Serve immediately.

tip If you don't have a green thumb, don't worry. You can still enjoy this tasty salad . . . just head to your closest farmers' market or organic grocery to pick up some "homegrown" veggies.

meze-in-a-minute platter

A popular way of eating in the Mediterranean and Middle East, a meze platter is a collection of small appetizers, salads, and dips. I like to throw this easy platter together when I have a few friends over or I feel like a snack.
MAKES 8 APPETIZER SALADS

1	bag (10 ounces) Hearts of Romaine
1	cup prepared tabbouleh (see tip on page 81)
1	cup prepared hummus
1	can (10 ounces) dolmas (about a dozen stuffed grape leaves)
1	cup brine-cured black olives
4	pita breads, cut into 6 wedges each

• Spread the Hearts of Romaine evenly across a large platter. Arrange the tabbouleh, hummus, dolmas, black olives, and pita wedges on the platter. Serve immediately.

tip The beauty of this no-fuss platter is that all the items can be picked up already prepared at your local grocery store or deli.

A perfect finger food, dolmas are a mixture of ground lamb, rice, and spices wrapped up in grape leaves. They are popular in Greek and Turkish cuisines.

panzanella

Originally invented by the Italians as a way to use up day-old bread, this salad is delicious no matter how old—or not—the bread is! **MAKES 6 APPETIZER OR SIDE SALADS**

salad . . . .

1	large ripe tomato, cut into 1-inch pieces
1	small cucumber, halved, seeded, and cut into ½-inch pieces
1	red bell pepper, seeded and cut into 1-inch pieces
1	yellow bell pepper, seeded and cut into 1-inch pieces
½	red onion, halved and thinly sliced
10	large basil leaves, sliced into thin strips
1	bag (7 ounces) Riviera™ Blend, torn into 1-inch pieces

• In a large salad bowl, toss together the tomato, cucumber, red bell pepper, yellow bell pepper, red onion, basil, and the Riviera Blend. Add the croutons and the vinaigrette to taste. Toss gently. Set aside to allow the croutons to soak up the vinaigrette, 10 to 20 minutes.

croutons . . . .

2	tablespoons extra-virgin olive oil
½	small loaf of French or Italian country bread (15 ounces), cut into 1-inch cubes

• In a large sauté pan over medium heat, warm the oil until a few water droplets sizzle in the pan. Add the bread and cook, stirring as needed, until golden brown, about 4 minutes. Using a slotted spoon transfer croutons to a paper towel–lined plate to drain. Cool to room temperature.

red wine-garlic vinaigrette . . . .

½	small garlic clove, mashed to a paste (see tip on page 230 for directions) or minced
2	tablespoons red wine vinegar
6	tablespoons extra-virgin olive oil
	Kosher salt and freshly ground pepper

• In a small bowl whisk together the garlic and vinegar. Slowly add the oil in a steady stream, whisking to emulsify. Season with salt and pepper to taste. **MAKES ABOUT ¼ CUP**

tip A quick trick to cut basil into thin strips, also known as a chiffonade, is to place clean leaves in a pile, roll the leaves lengthwise like a cigarette, and thinly slice the roll crosswise.

warm wild mushroom salad
with sherry vinaigrette

The earthy flavors of wild mushrooms are so deliciously intense. After enjoying this salad, you may never eat a common mushroom again. **MAKES 6 APPETIZER OR 4 DINNER SALADS**

¼	cup Sherry Vinaigrette (see page 106)
¼	pound pancetta, diced
1	shallot, minced
½	pound assorted wild mushrooms, such as chanterelle, trumpet, and porcini, ends trimmed
½	cup pine nuts, toasted
	Kosher salt and freshly ground pepper
1	bag (8 ounces) Field Greens

• Prepare the Sherry Vinaigrette.

• In a medium skillet over medium-low heat, cook the pancetta until crisp, about 4 minutes. Transfer the pancetta to a paper towel–lined plate to drain, reserving the drippings in the pan. Increase the heat to medium. Add the shallot and cook, stirring often, until tender, 3 to 5 minutes. Add the mushrooms and cook, stirring often, until lightly browned, about 5 minutes. Transfer the mixture to a medium bowl. Add the pancetta and pine nuts to the mushroom mixture and toss. Season with salt and pepper to taste.

• In a large salad bowl, toss the Field Greens with the vinaigrette to taste. Divide the salad among individual plates. Top with the warm mushrooms. Serve immediately.

tip If fresh wild mushrooms are not available, substitute dried mushrooms. Reconstitute as per the package directions and voilá . . . you have delicious mushrooms for your salad.

crunchy asian salad

Combining traditional greens with a crunchy slaw, this Asian salad is bursting with strong flavors and textures.
MAKES 8 SIDE SALADS

½	cup Peanut Dressing (see page 234)
1	bag (10 ounces) Hearts of Romaine
1	bag (10 ounces) Angel Hair Cole Slaw
3	carrots, peeled, halved lengthwise, and sliced into thin matchsticks
½	cup thinly sliced scallions
¼	cup coarsely chopped fresh cilantro leaves
¾	cup rice noodles
	Kosher salt and freshly ground pepper

• Prepare the Peanut Dressing.

• In a large bowl toss together the Hearts of Romaine, Angel Hair Cole Slaw, carrots, scallions, cilantro, and rice noodles. Add the dressing to taste and gently toss. Season with salt and pepper to taste. Serve immediately.

tip   To easily cut the carrots into thin matchsticks, also known as julienne, use a mandoline. A mandoline is a manual kitchen utensil that can be used to thinly slice, julienne, shred, or waffle cut vegetables. In addition to the traditional French varieties, there are now ten-dollar Asian varieties available in Asian supermarkets.

insalata primavera

Inspired by a salad that I enjoyed in a little Italian restaurant in New York, this delicious salad is light and flavorful. **MAKES 6 APPETIZER OR SIDE SALADS**

¼	cup Red Wine Dijon Vinaigrette (see page 61)
1	bag (8 ounces) Triple Hearts™
¼	red onion, very thinly sliced
¼	cup red pear tomatoes, halved
¼	cup yellow pear tomatoes, halved
¼	pound ricotta salata, cut into pea-size cubes
2	tablespoons capers, drained and rinsed
	Kosher salt and freshly ground pepper

• Prepare the Red Wine Dijon Vinaigrette.

• In a large salad bowl, toss together the Triple Hearts, red onion, red and yellow tomatoes, ricotta salata, and capers. Add the vinaigrette to taste and gently toss. Season with salt and pepper to taste.

tip Perfect for dicing or crumbling over salads, ricotta salata is an Italian salted sheep's milk cheese with a smooth, firm texture. Feta cheese is the best substitute if you can't find the tangy ricotta salata.

roasted beet salad
with goat cheese, candied walnuts, and citrus vinaigrette

Roasting beets brings out their natural sweet and earthy flavor. They will taste nothing like the canned beets that you find in the self-serve salad bar. MAKES 4 DINNER OR 6 APPETIZER SALADS

salad . . . .

¼	pound small to medium beets, stems trimmed and scrubbed
1	bag (5 ounces) Sweet Baby Greens
1	log (4 ounces) fresh goat cheese
¼	cup candied walnuts

• Preheat the oven to 400°F. Wrap the beets in aluminum foil. Place foil packet on a rimmed baking pan and bake until the tip of a sharp knife easily slides through the beets, about 45 minutes to 1 hour. Remove from the oven and cool. Once cool enough to handle, use paper towels to peel the beets. Cut into quarters.

• Divide Sweet Baby Greens equally among the plates. Top with the beets. Drizzle with the vinaigrette to taste. Crumble the goat cheese on top and garnish with the candied walnuts.

candied walnuts . . . .

1	cup shelled walnut halves
¼	cup sugar
1	teaspoon kosher salt

• Preheat the oven to 325°F.

• Spread the nuts evenly on a nonstick rimmed baking pan with sides and place in the oven. Toast, stirring occasionally, until golden and fragrant, about 3 minutes. Remove from the oven and let cool in the pan.

• Place the sugar in a medium saucepan over medium-low heat. Slowly cook, stirring frequently, until melted and turned a light caramel color. Remove from the heat and immediately add the walnuts to the saucepan, stirring to coat.

• Spread the coated walnuts back out onto the same baking pan. Working quickly, separate the walnuts to create an even layer. Lightly sprinkle with the salt. Set aside to cool completely. Candied walnuts can be stored up to two days in an airtight container. MAKES ABOUT 1 CUP

tip Candied nuts are often available prepacked in the grocery store.

citrus vinaigrette . . . .

½   shallot, minced

1   tablespoon freshly squeezed lemon juice

3   tablespoons freshly squeezed orange juice

1   teaspoon finely grated orange zest

½   teaspoon Dijon mustard

2   tablespoons extra-virgin olive oil
     Kosher salt and freshly ground pepper

• In small bowl whisk together the shallot, lemon juice, orange juice, orange zest, Dijon mustard, and oil until well combined. Season with salt and pepper to taste. MAKES ABOUT ¼ CUP

grilled vegetable salad

There is something about the smoky, charred flavor of grilled vegetables that is hard to resist.

MAKES 4 DINNER OR 6 APPETIZER SALADS

salad . . . .

1	zucchini, cut lengthwise and then into ½-inch slices
1	yellow squash, cut lengthwise and then into ½-inch slices
1	small eggplant, cut into 1-inch cubes
1	red bell pepper, seeded and cut into 1-inch squares
1	red onion, cut into ½-inch thick slices
1	tablespoon dried Italian seasoning
	Kosher salt and freshly ground pepper
1	bag (10 ounces) Hearts of Romaine
	Parmesan shavings, for garnish

• Preheat a clean grill to medium.

• In a large bowl toss the zucchini, squash, eggplant, red bell pepper, red onion, Italian seasoning, and ¼ cup of the vinaigrette until well coated. Marinate for 30 minutes.

• Season the vegetables with salt and pepper. Transfer the vegetables, shaking off the excess marinade, to a grill basket and grill until slightly charred, about 10 minutes per side. Place in a large salad bowl and let cool to room temperature.

• Add the Hearts of Romaine to the cooked vegetables and toss. Add the remaining vinaigrette to taste and gently toss. Divide among individual plates. Garnish with the Parmesan cheese shavings. Serve immediately.

balsamic vinaigrette . . . .

¼	cup balsamic vinegar
¾	cup extra-virgin olive oil
	Kosher salt and freshly ground pepper

• Place the vinegar in a small bowl. Slowly add the oil in a steady stream, whisking to emulsify. Season with salt and pepper to taste. MAKES ABOUT 1 CUP

tip Grilling baskets help keep small cut vegetables from falling through the grates. If you don't own one, cut the vegetables into large pieces that are too big to fall through the grates. Once cool enough to handle, cut into bite-size portions. Another option is to cook them in a grill pan.

hearts of palm salad
with red onion vinaigrette

Harvested from the inner core of palm trees, hearts of palm are tender and delicate. **Makes 6 appetizer salads**

salad . . . .

1	bag (5 ounces) Sweet Baby Lettuces
1	can (14 ounces) hearts of palm, drained and sliced diagonally
1	red bell pepper, seeded and finely diced

• Divide the Sweet Baby Lettuces equally among individual plates. Arrange the hearts of palm on top. Spoon the vinaigrette over the top. Garnish with the red bell pepper.

red onion vinaigrette . . . .

2	tablespoons white balsamic vinegar
1	tablespoon whole-grain Dijon mustard
1	garlic clove, minced
6	tablespoons extra-virgin olive oil
	Kosher salt and freshly ground pepper
½	medium red onion, thinly sliced into rings

• In a small bowl whisk together the vinegar, mustard, and garlic. Slowly add the oil in a steady stream, whisking to emulsify. Season with salt and pepper to taste.

• Add the onion and toss to coat. Refrigerate for 30 minutes to marinate the onion.
Makes about ½ cup

tip Hearts of palm are most commonly found in cans or jars in the canned vegetable section of grocery stores near the artichoke hearts.

CHAPTER SIX

fruit

mango, avocado, and cilantro salad

My Nicaraguan friend, Lucia Heros, serves this refreshing salad of mango, avocado, and cilantro with her spicy Latin dishes. It is also a great accompaniment for grilled meat and seafood. **MAKES 6 APPETIZER OR SIDE SALADS**

¼	cup White Balsamic Vinaigrette (see page 7)
1	bag (5 ounces) Spring Mix
2	ripe avocados, peeled and diced
1	mango, seeded, diced, and peeled (see tip on page 94 for instructions)
½	red onion, finely diced
½	cup fresh cilantro leaves

• Prepare the White Balsamic Vinaigrette.

• In a large salad bowl, toss together the Spring Mix, avocados, mango, red onion, and cilantro. Add the vinaigrette to taste and gently toss. Serve immediately.

tip To prevent the avocado from turning brown, prepare just before serving and drizzle with lime juice.

english farmhouse salad

The tart flavor of the Granny Smith apples is a great complement to the sweet cider vinaigrette and the pungent Stilton in this salad. **MAKES 6 APPETIZER OR SIDE SALADS**

salad . . . .

1	Granny Smith apple, cored and thinly sliced
1	tablespoon canola or vegetable oil
1	bag (5 ounces) Spring Mix
½	cup walnuts, toasted and cooled
½	cup crumbled Stilton blue cheese

• Preheat a clean grill or grill pan to medium low. In a medium bowl toss the apple slices with the oil until well coated. Place the apple slices in a grilling basket and grill until just softened, about 2 minutes per side. Set aside to cool.

• In a large salad bowl, toss the Spring Mix, walnuts, and Stilton cheese. Add the vinaigrette to taste and gently toss. Top with grilled apple slices.

apple cider vinaigrette . . . .

5	tablespoons sugar
¼	teaspoon dry mustard
5	tablespoons distilled white vinegar
3	teaspoons apple cider vinegar
1½	tablespoons Worcestershire sauce
3	tablespoons canola oil
	Kosher salt and freshly ground black pepper

• In a small bowl whisk together the sugar, dry mustard, white vinegar, apple cider vinegar, and Worcestershire sauce until the sugar has dissolved. Slowly add the oil in a stream, whisking to emulsify. Season with salt and pepper to taste. **MAKES ABOUT ½ CUP**

tip Hailed by some as the "king of blue cheeses," Stilton is a pungent cheese produced in England since the 1700s. Fresh Stilton, as with any fresh blue cheese, will have a much stronger flavor than the supermarket packages of precrumbled blue cheeses.

balsamic strawberry salad

The balsamic vinegar enhances the flavor of the strawberries and adds depth to this delicious fruit. If you have any marinated berries left over, spoon them over vanilla ice cream for a tasty dessert.

MAKES 6 APPETIZER OR SIDE SALADS

¼   cup Balsamic Vinaigrette (see page 120)
½   pint fresh strawberries, hulled and thinly sliced
1   tablespoon balsamic vinegar
1   bag (5 ounces) Baby Arugula
½   cup pecan halves, toasted
      Kosher salt and freshly ground pepper

• Prepare the Balsamic Vinaigrette.

• In a large salad bowl, toss the strawberries with the balsamic vinegar.
Marinate for 10 minutes.

• Add the Baby Arugula and pecan halves to the marinated strawberries.
Add the vinaigrette to taste and gently toss. Season with salt and pepper to taste.
Serve immediately.

tip Hulling a strawberry is a fancy way to say "removing the green stem." If
you don't have the special strawberry huller tool, just insert a paring knife
at a 45-degee angle at the base of the stem. Carefully twist until the stem
is removed. Using this technique, you only remove the stem and none of
the sweet juicy flesh.

pear and spinach salad

The sweet flesh of the pear is the perfect complement to tasty greens and pungent Gorgonzola blue cheese.

MAKES 6 APPETIZER OR SIDE SALADS

¼	cup Basic Vinaigrette (see page 228)
2	pears (preferably Bosc)
1	bag (6 ounces) Baby Spinach
¼	pound Gorgonzola, thinly sliced
¼	cup almond slices, toasted

• Prepare the Basic Vinaigrette.

• Peel the pears. Using a vegetable peeler, shave the pear meat into thin slivers.

• Place the Baby Spinach in a large salad bowl. Add the vinaigrette to taste and gently toss to coat. Divide the spinach among the plates. Top with the pear shavings and Gorgonzola slices. Sprinkle with the almonds. Serve immediately.

tip Do not peel and slice the pear until just before serving or it may brown. If you must prepare the pears in advance, soak in acidulated water (water with a little lemon juice) to help prevent browning. The basic recipe is 1 tablespoon lemon juice to 1 cup room temperature water.

orange and fennel salad

Similar in taste to licorice, fennel adds an interesting twist to this sweet and savory salad.
Makes 6 appetizer or side salads

4	oranges, peeled
2	fennel bulbs, trimmed, cored, and thinly sliced lengthwise
2	tablespoons Kalamata or Niçoise olives, pitted
1	bag (5 ounces) Baby Lettuces
2	tablespoons extra-virgin olive oil
	Kosher salt and freshly ground pepper

• Over a large salad bowl, separate the orange slices, catching the juice in the bowl. Remove the seeds. Add the orange slices to the bowl. Add the fennel, olives, Baby Lettuces, and oil and gently toss. Season with salt and pepper to taste.

tip To trim and core a bulb of fennel, cut off the stalks from the top of the bulb and remove any tough outer layers. Cut the bulb into quarters and remove the hard core with a paring knife.

watermelon and arugula salad

Juicy, refreshing watermelon tossed with spicy arugula is the prefect summertime backyard barbecue treat.

MAKES 6 APPETIZER OR SIDE SALADS

salad . . . .

1	bag (5 ounces) Baby Arugula
1	small watermelon, seeded and cut into 1-inch cubes
¼	cup crumbled feta cheese
¼	cup pine nuts, toasted (see tip on page 91)

• In a large salad bowl, toss the Baby Arugula, watermelon, feta cheese, and pine nuts. Add the vinaigrette to taste and gently toss.

vinaigrette . . . .

1	tablespoon freshly squeezed lemon juice
1	tablespoon red wine vinegar
4	tablespoons extra-virgin olive oil
	Kosher salt and freshly ground pepper

• In a small bowl whisk together the lemon juice and red wine vinegar. Slowly add the oil in a steady stream, whisking to emulsify. Season with salt and pepper to taste. MAKES ABOUT ½ CUP

tip Add fresh mint leaves for an interesting zing to this refreshing salad.

grapefruit and avocado salad

Top this salad with grilled shrimp for a tropical delight. **MAKES 6 APPETIZER OR SIDE SALADS**

1	grapefruit, peeled
½	white onion, halved and thinly sliced
2	ripe avocados, halved, peeled, and cut into thin slices
1	bag (7 ounces) Riviera™ Blend
3	tablespoons extra-virgin olive oil
	Kosher salt and freshly ground pepper

• Over a large salad bowl, separate the grapefruit slices, catching the juice in the bowl. Remove the seeds. Add the grapefruit slices to the bowl. Add the onion, avocados, Riviera Blend, and olive oil and gently toss. Season with salt and pepper to taste.

tip Want juicy and colorful grapefruit or orange slices for your salads? Remove the peel with a sharp knife, being sure to remove all of the white pith. Then cut between the membranes to separate the segments. Before discarding, squeeze the remaining membranes over the bowl to capture all the luscious juices for your dressing.

arugula salad
with goat cheese-stuffed figs and fig vinaigrette

I first had this salad years ago at a little Italian restaurant in San Francisco. I have long since forgotten the name of the place, but I have not forgotten to make this tasty salad each year when fresh figs are in season.
MAKES 6 APPETIZER SALADS

salad . . . .

1	tablespoon extra-virgin olive oil
1	log (10.5 ounces) goat cheese, sliced in tablespoon portions
12	fresh figs, halved lengthwise
½	pound pancetta, thinly sliced (at least 12 slices)
12	wooden toothpicks, soaked in water for at least one hour
1	bag (5 ounces) Baby Arugula

• Preheat the oven to 375°F. Grease a rimmed baking pan with the oil.

• Place 1 tablespoon goat cheese in between two fig halves. Wrap the halves together with a slice of pancetta and secure with a wooden toothpick. Place the figs on the prepared baking pan. Repeat the process with the remaining figs. Bake until the pancetta has turned slightly crispy, about 12 minutes. Cool slightly and remove the toothpicks.

• Divide the Baby Arugula among individual plates and top with 2 baked figs. Lightly drizzle with the vinaigrette to taste.

fig vinaigrette . . . .

2	tablespoons black fig vinegar
½	teaspoon Dijon mustard
6	tablespoons extra-virgin olive oil
	Kosher salt and freshly ground pepper

• In a small bowl whisk together the vinegar and mustard. Slowly add the oil in a steady stream, whisking to emulsify. Season with salt and pepper to taste. MAKES ABOUT ¼ CUP

tip Fruit-infused vinegars, such as black fig vinegar, are available in most gourmet markets or for order on-line.

waldorf salad

Originally created at New York City's Waldorf-Astoria Hotel back in the 1890s, this salad of apples, celery, and mayonnaise has been a favorite ever since. **MAKES 6 APPETIZER OR SIDE SALADS**

2	Fuji apples, cored and cut in half
1	Red Delicious apple, cored and cut in half
3	tablespoons apple cider vinegar
¾	cup walnuts, toasted and coarsely chopped
1	cup golden raisins
2	teaspoons curry powder
2	stalks celery, thinly sliced on the bias
⅓	cup fresh mint, cut into thin strips
½	red onion, halved and thinly sliced
1	cup mayonnaise
	Kosher salt and freshly ground pepper
1	bag (10 ounces) Hearts of Romaine

• Leaving the skin on for color, chop the apples into ¼-inch pieces. In a large salad bowl, toss the apples with the cider vinegar. Add the walnuts, raisins, curry powder, celery, mint, and red onion and toss. Fold in the mayonnaise, to taste, to evenly coat. Season with salt and pepper to taste. Cover and refrigerate until the flavors have melded, at least 1 hour. To serve, arrange the Hearts of Romaine on individual plates and spoon the apple mixture on top.

tip You can easily turn this light salad into an entrée by adding diced chicken or turkey to the apple mixture.

fresh fruit salad
with poppy seed dressing

Serve this light and fruity salad for a ladies' luncheon with orange blossom or lemon poppy seed mini muffins.
MAKES 4 DINNER OR 6 APPETIZER SALADS

salad . . . .

½	cantaloupe, peeled, seeded and diced
½	honeydew melon, peeled, seeded and diced
½	cup fresh strawberries, hulled and thinly sliced
½	cup fresh raspberries
¼	cup fresh blueberries
1	bag (8 ounces) Triple Hearts™

• In a large salad bowl, gently toss together the cantaloupe, honeydew melon, strawberries, raspberries, and blueberries. Add the dressing to taste and gently toss to coat.

• To serve, arrange the Triple Hearts on individual plates and top with a generous spoonful of the fruit salad.

poppy seed dressing . . . .

3	tablespoons red wine vinegar
⅓	cup sugar
1	teaspoon dry mustard
¾	teaspoon kosher salt
⅓	cup vegetable oil
1	tablespoon poppy seeds

• In a blender combine the vinegar, sugar, dry mustard, salt, and oil. Purée until well combined. Fold in the poppy seeds. MAKES ABOUT 1 CUP

tip For a quick alternative, whip up a creamy vanilla-honey dressing for your fruit salad. Whisk together 1 cup vanilla yogurt with 1 tablespoon honey and a dash of ground cinnamon.

hearts of romaine
with tart apples, hazelnuts, and sharp cheddar cheese

This salad is a great example of how using good quality, simple ingredients can make something out of the ordinary. Serve this salad at your next backyard barbecue. **MAKES 6 APPETIZER OR SIDE SALADS**

¼	cup Sherry Vinaigrette (see page 106)
1	bag (10 ounces) Hearts of Romaine
2	Granny Smith apples, cored, halved, and thinly sliced
½	cup hazelnuts, toasted and skinned
½	cup coarsely shredded sharp Cheddar cheese

• Prepare the Sherry Vinaigrette.

• In a large salad bowl, toss together the Hearts of Romaine, apples, hazelnuts, and cheese. Add the vinaigrette to taste and gently toss. Serve immediately.

tip To skin hazelnuts, spread them evenly on a baking sheet. Toast in a 350°F oven until fragrant and skins begin to crack, about 10 minutes. Remove from the oven and roll the nuts in a clean, rough-textured towel or paper towel until the skins flake off.

Using prepacked shredded Cheddar cheese saves time, but you will get much more flavor shredding a good sharp Cheddar yourself.

mixed lettuces
with strawberries, red grapes, and almonds

Barbara Hanemann, my wonderful mom, serves this sweet and savory salad for her investment club get-togethers.
MAKES 6 APPETIZER OR SIDE SALADS

salad . . . .

1	bag (8 ounces) Mediterranean Blend
½	pint fresh strawberries, hulled and thinly sliced
⅔	cup red grapes, halved
¼	cup thinly sliced scallions
¼	cup sliced almonds, toasted
¼	cup crumbled blue cheese (preferably Maytag)
	Kosher salt and freshly ground pepper

• In a large salad bowl, toss together the Mediterranean Blend, strawberries, grapes, scallions, almond slices, and crumbled blue cheese. Add the dressing to taste and gently toss. Season with salt and pepper to taste.

blush wine vinaigrette . . . .

3	tablespoons red wine vinegar
2	tablespoons freshly squeezed lemon juice
2	tablespoons sugar
5	tablespoons canola oil
	Kosher salt and freshly ground pepper

• In a small bowl whisk together the vinegar, lemon juice, and sugar until the sugar has dissolved. Slowly add the oil in a stream, whisking to emulsify. Season with salt and pepper to taste. MAKES ABOUT ½ CUP

tip   Mix and match this colorful salad using your favorite ingredients. Try substituting spinach for the Mediterranean Blend or using green grapes or dried cranberries.

wild berry salad

This colorful salad combines the sweet and the savory perfectly together. **MAKES 6 APPETIZER OR SIDE SALADS**

salad . . . .

1	bag (10 ounces) Baby Spinach
½	cup fresh blueberries
½	cup fresh raspberries
½	cup fresh blackberries
½	cup hulled and quartered fresh strawberries
	Kosher salt and freshly ground pepper

• In a large salad bowl, toss together the Baby Spinach, blueberries, raspberries, blackberries, and strawberries. Add the dressing to taste and gently toss. Season with salt and pepper to taste. Serve immediately.

fresh raspberry dressing . . . .

½	cup fresh raspberries or frozen unsweetened raspberries
1	tablespoon apple juice
2	tablespoons raspberry balsamic vinegar
1¼	tablespoons water
1	tablespoon sugar
2	tablespoons canola oil
	Kosher salt and freshly ground pepper

• Place the raspberries, apple juice, vinegar, water, sugar, and oil in a blender. Purée until smooth. Season with salt and pepper to taste.
MAKES ABOUT ¾ CUP

tip Toasted pine nuts or sunflower seeds would make a nice "crunchy" addition to this salad. Also consider adding crumbled goat cheese.

Tropical Fruit Salad
with Passion Fruit Vinaigrette

This salad makes me dream of the Caribbean. The dressing, made primarily of fruit juice, adds a sweet but light fruitiness to the bitter arugula greens. **MAKES 6 TO 8 APPETIZER SALADS**

salad . . . .

1	bag (5 ounces) Baby Arugula
3	tablespoons coarsely chopped fresh mint leaves
1	mango, peeled, pitted, and sliced lengthwise
1	small papaya, cut in half lengthwise, seeded, peeled, and sliced lengthwise
8	pineapple slices (fresh or canned), cut in half

• In a large salad bowl, place the Baby Arugula and mint leaves. Add the dressing to taste and gently toss. Arrange the slices of mango, papaya, and pineapple on individual plates. Top with the salad. Serve immediately.

passion fruit dressing . . . .

6	tablespoons medley of tropical fruit juice (must include passion fruit juice)
1	tablespoon minced shallot
2	tablespoons extra-virgin olive oil
	Kosher salt

• In a small bowl whisk together the juice, shallot, and oil until well combined. Season with salt to taste. MAKES ABOUT ¼ CUP

tip Substitute any tropical fruit, such as kiwi or guava, that is available at your local market. Simply combine your favorite fruit juices into a glass and use what you need and enjoy the remaining juice as a beverage.

CHAPTER SEVEN

beans, grains, rice & pasta

cheese tortellini salad
with sun-dried tomato vinaigrette

Zesty sun-dried tomatoes add a bold taste to this salad. **MAKES 4 DINNER SALADS**

salad ....

1	package (9 ounces) fresh three-cheese tortellini (available in the refrigerated pasta section)
1	tablespoon olive oil
1	bag (10 ounces) Italian Blend
¼	cup drained oil-packed sun-dried tomatoes, cut into thin strips
5	fresh basil leaves, sliced into thin strips

• Cook the pasta in a large pot of boiling salted water, according to package instructions, about 10 minutes. Drain and rinse under cold water until cool. Drizzle with the oil and toss to evenly coat to prevent sticking.

• Tear the Italian Blend into bite-size pieces and place in a large salad bowl. Add the tortellini and sun-dried tomatoes. Toss with the vinaigrette, to taste, until coated. Garnish with the basil.

sun-dried tomato vinaigrette ....

¼	cup drained oil-packed sun-dried tomatoes
4	teaspoons balsamic vinegar
4	teaspoons red wine vinegar
1	small garlic clove, minced
⅓	cup extra-virgin olive oil
	Kosher salt and freshly ground pepper

• Place the sun-dried tomatoes, balsamic vinegar, red wine vinegar, and garlic in a blender or food processor and purée until smooth. Gradually add the oil until emulsified. Season with salt and pepper to taste. MAKES ABOUT ¾ CUP

tip If you can only find dehydrated sun-dried tomatoes, no problem. Just reconstitute them in boiling water as per the package directions.

asian noodle salad with peanut dressing

Cool noodle salads are the perfect treat for a warm night. But be forewarned—they're addictive!

MAKES 4 DINNER OR 6 SIDE SALADS

½	cup Peanut Dressing (see page 234)
1	package (8 ounces) wide Chinese lo mein noodles
1	tablespoon toasted sesame oil
1	bag (10 ounces) Hearts of Romaine
4	scallions, sliced ½-inch long on the diagonal
1	carrot, peeled and grated on the large holes of a traditional grater
½	red bell pepper, seeded and thinly sliced

• Prepare the Peanut Dressing.

• Bring a large pot of salted water to a boil. Add the noodles and cook according to package instructions until al dente, about 10 minutes. Drain and rinse under cold water to cool. Place the drained noodles in a large salad bowl, and toss with the toasted sesame oil to prevent sticking.

• Add the Hearts of Romaine, scallions, carrot, and red bell pepper to the noodles. Drizzle with the Peanut Dressing to taste and toss to combine.

tip For a heartier dish, toss in some cooked shredded chicken.

lentil and tri-color pepper salad

With a distinctive earthy flavor, lentils are easier and faster to cook than other dried beans. The cumin dressing in this recipe enhances their flavor. **MAKES 4 DINNER OR 6 SIDE SALADS**

salad ....

1	yellow bell pepper
1	red bell pepper
1	orange bell pepper
1¼	cups lentils, rinsed and drained
3	cups water
½	yellow onion, peeled
1	garlic clove, peeled
	Kosher salt and freshly ground pepper
½	red onion, thinly sliced
1	bag (6 ounces) Baby Spinach

• To roast the peppers, heat a clean grill to high heat. Lay the peppers on the grate and cook until well charred. Rotate the peppers a quarter turn and repeat until each side is well charred. Place the charred, hot peppers in a resealable bag. Seal and steam until cooled to room temperature, about 30 minutes. Remove the peppers from the bag and, using a paper towel, remove the skin. Gently pull the peppers apart and remove and discard the seeds and stems. Thinly slice the peppers.

• In a large saucepan combine the lentils, water, yellow onion, and garlic and bring to a boil. Reduce the heat and simmer, uncovered, until the lentils are tender but still holding their shape, 20 to 25 minutes. Drain the lentils and transfer to a large bowl; discard the onion and garlic clove.

• Pour the dressing over the warm lentils to taste and stir to combine. Season with salt and pepper to taste. Set aside to cool to room temperature.

• Stir the sliced peppers and red onion into the cooled lentils. Divide the Baby Spinach among individual plates. Top with a generous spoonful of lentils. Serve immediately.

dressing ....

2	tablespoons freshly squeezed lemon juice
1	small garlic clove, minced
½	teaspoon ground cumin
¼	cup extra-virgin olive oil
1	tablespoon coarsely chopped fresh cilantro leaves

• In a small bowl whisk together the lemon juice, garlic, cumin, oil, and cilantro. MAKES ABOUT ¼ CUP tip Pouring the dressing over the warm lentils ensures that they will soak up the maximum amount of flavor. If you do not have a grill, you can char your peppers in your oven at 450°F or over the flame of a gas burner.

brown rice, corn, and grilled vegetable salad

The smoky flavor of the grilled vegetables is the key to this healthy salad. **MAKES 6 DINNER OR 8 SIDE SALADS**

salad . . . .

1	zucchini, cut lengthwise and sliced into ¼-inch pieces
1	red bell pepper, seeded and cut into 1-inch squares
1	red onion, cut into ½-inch slices
¼	cup extra-virgin olive oil
2	tablespoons soy sauce
2	ears corn, shucked
	Kosher salt and freshly ground pepper
1	cup brown rice, cooked and cooled to room temperature
1	bag (10 ounces) Hearts of Romaine

• Preheat a clean grill to medium.

• In a large bowl toss the zucchini, red bell pepper, red onion, oil, and soy sauce until well coated. Marinate for 30 minutes.

• Wrap the corn in aluminum foil and grill until tender, about 10 minutes. When cool enough to handle, slice the corn kernels from the cob. Put the corn kernels in a large salad bowl. Discard the cobs.

• Season the vegetables with salt and pepper. Transfer the vegetables, without excess marinade, to a grilling basket and grill until slightly charred, about 10 minutes per side. Discard the marinade. Combine the grilled vegetables with the corn. Let cool to room temperature.

• Add the cooked rice and Hearts of Romaine to the vegetable mixture and toss. Add the dressing to taste and toss to coat. Season with salt and pepper to taste.

dressing . . . .

½	cup freshly squeezed orange juice
1	tablespoon freshly squeezed lemon juice
2	tablespoons soy sauce
2	tablespoons extra-virgin olive oil

• In a small bowl whisk together the orange juice, lemon juice, soy sauce, and oil until well combined. **MAKES ABOUT ¾ CUP**

tip   If you don't have an outdoor grill, sear the vegetables in a cast-iron skillet or a grill pan.

cannellini bean and roasted red pepper salad

On a trip to Italy many years ago, I enjoyed this light salad for lunch. Popular in Italian cooking, cannellini beans are also known as white kidney beans. **MAKES 6 APPETIZER OR SIDE SALADS**

salad . . . .

1	lemon
1	can (15 ounces) cannellini beans, rinsed and drained
1	roasted red bell pepper (see page 176 for roasting instructions), cut into thin strips (about ½ cup)
1	bag (5 ounces) Baby Arugula
	Kosher salt and freshly ground pepper

• Using a vegetable peeler, in a top to bottom motion, peel the rind from the lemon in long strips. Cut lengthwise into very thin strips. Or use the large hole on the side of a zester. Juice the lemon, refrigerate, and save for another use.

• In a large salad bowl, toss together the cannellini beans, red bell pepper, Baby Arugula, and lemon strips. Add the vinaigrette to taste and gently toss. Season with salt and pepper to taste. Serve immediately.

red wine vinaigrette . . . .

2	tablespoons red wine vinegar
6	tablespoons extra-virgin olive oil
	Kosher salt and freshly ground pepper

• Place the vinegar in a small bowl. Slowly add the oil in a stream, whisking to emulsify. Season with salt and pepper to taste. MAKES ABOUT ¼ CUP

tip When peeling the lemon, try to only remove the outer yellow part of the peel. The white pithy part underneath has a bitter flavor.

curried rice and chickpea salad

Inspired by a dish served at one of my favorite health food stores, this salad is a perfect accompaniment for grilled lamb kabobs. **MAKES 4 DINNER OR 6 SIDE SALADS**

salad

1	cup brown rice, cooked and cooled to room temperature
1	can (15 ounces) chickpeas, rinsed and drained
1	bag (8 ounces) Shredded Lettuce
½	red bell pepper, seeded and finely chopped
2	tablespoons slivered almonds, toasted
	Kosher salt and freshly ground pepper

• In a large salad bowl, toss together the brown rice, chickpeas, Shredded Lettuce, red bell pepper, and almonds. Add the dressing to taste and gently toss. Season with salt and pepper to taste. Serve immediately.

curry dressing

¼	cup freshly squeezed orange juice
2	tablespoons white wine vinegar
3	tablespoons extra-virgin olive oil
½	teaspoon curry powder

• In a small bowl whisk together the orange juice, vinegar, oil, and curry powder until well combined. **MAKES ABOUT ½ CUP**

tip Chickpeas are also commonly labeled as garbanzo beans.

grilled portobello and couscous salad

Featuring the "steak" of the mushroom family, this meatless main course is sure to please. **MAKES 4 DINNER SALADS**

¼	cup Red Wine Vinaigrette (see page 180)		1	carrot, peeled and finely diced
4	large portobello mushrooms caps, cleaned		½	red bell pepper, seeded and finely diced
2	tablespoons extra-virgin olive oil		¼	red onion, finely diced
	Kosher salt and freshly ground pepper		½	zucchini, finely diced
1	cup plain couscous, cooked and cooled to room temperature		1	bag (8 ounces) Triple Hearts™

• Prepare the Red Wine Vinaigrette.

• Preheat a clean grill or grill pan to medium high.

• Brush the portobello mushrooms with the oil and season with salt and pepper. Grill until fork tender, about 3 minutes per side. Set aside to cool to room temperature. Cut into ½-inch slices.

• In a large salad bowl, toss together the prepared couscous, carrot, red bell pepper, onion, and zucchini. Add the vinaigrette to taste, reserving some to drizzle over the Triple Hearts, and gently toss to coat. Season with salt and pepper to taste.

• Divide the Triple Hearts among the plates. Drizzle with the remaining vinaigrette. Top with a generous spoonful of the couscous mixture. Arrange the portobello slices across the top. Serve immediately.

tip Couscous is a grain that has a pebble-like texture and nutty flavor when cooked. It is a cinch to prepare. Just pour boiling water over the uncooked grain, cover, and set aside until the grains have expanded, about 5 minutes. And, without really cooking, you are done.

summer bean salad

Tender and sweet, yellow wax beans are a delightful summertime treat. **MAKES 6 SIDE SALADS**

¼   cup Lemon Vinaigrette (see page 231)

¾   pound yellow wax beans, stem ends trimmed

¾   cup cherry tomatoes, halved crosswise

½   cup Kalamata olives, pitted and halved

       Kosher salt and freshly ground pepper

1   bag (5 ounces) Sweet Baby Greens

• Prepare the Lemon Vinaigrette.

• Bring a large pot of salted water to a boil. Add the beans, return to a boil, and cook until just tender, about 2 minutes more. Drain the beans and rinse with cold water until cooled.

• In a large salad bowl, toss together the beans, tomatoes, and olives. Add the vinaigrette to taste and gently toss to coat. Season with salt and pepper to taste.

• Arrange the Sweet Baby Greens among individual plates. Top with a generous spoonful of the bean salad. Serve immediately.

tip Since yellow wax beans are only available a few months per year, this salad can be made using green beans as well.

baked polenta salad
topped with goat cheese and fresh herbs

My good friend Fontaine Brown often serves this delectable dinner salad when she hosts our monthly book club.
MAKES 6 DINNER SALADS

¼	cup Balsamic Grainy Mustard Vinaigrette (see page 229)		¼	cup grated Parmesan cheese
				Kosher salt and freshly ground pepper
1	tablespoon extra-virgin olive oil		1	bag (5 ounces) Fresh Herb Blend
3	cups water		1	red bell pepper, seeded and finely diced
¾	cup uncooked polenta		1	cup crumbled goat cheese
2	tablespoons butter			

• Prepare the Balsamic Grainy Mustard Vinaigrette.

• Preheat the oven to 375°F. Lightly grease an 8-inch square baking pan with the oil. Set aside.

• In a medium pot, bring the water to a boil. Whisk in the polenta and stir. Reduce the heat and simmer, stirring often, until the mixture thickens and the polenta is tender. Remove from the heat and stir in the butter and Parmesan cheese until melted. Season with salt and pepper to taste. Pour into the prepared pan, spreading evenly. Transfer to the oven. Bake until golden and firm, about 15 minutes. Set aside until cool enough to handle, but still warm.

• Place the Fresh Herb Blend in a large salad bowl. Add the vinaigrette to taste and gently toss. Divide the salad among the plates.

• Cut the polenta into 6 rectangles. Place a piece of polenta on each plate. Garnish with the red pepper and goat cheese. Serve immediately.

tip Baked polenta can make a great presentation. I used rectangles in this recipe, but feel free to use cookie cutters to cut it in different shapes.

mediterranean pasta salad

The ingredients in this salad are all indigenous to the sunny Mediterranean coast line.

MAKES 6 DINNER OR 8 SIDE SALADS

salad . . . .

1	box (16 ounces) rotelle pasta
½	cup pepperoncinis, drained, stemmed, and coarsely chopped
½	cup Kalamata olives, pitted
½	cup drained oil-packed sun-dried tomatoes, cut into thin julienne strips
1	roasted red bell pepper (see page 176 for roasting instructions), cut into thin strips (about ½ cup)
1	jar (4 ounces) marinated artichoke hearts, drained and coarsely chopped
1	bag (5 ounces) Baby Arugula
	Kosher salt and freshly ground pepper

• Prepare the pasta as per the directions on the package. Rinse under cold water and drain thoroughly.

• In a large salad bowl, place the pasta, pepperoncinis, olives, sun-dried tomatoes, roasted red pepper, artichoke hearts, and Baby Arugula. Add the vinaigrette to taste and gently toss to combine. Season with salt and pepper to taste. Serve immediately.

vinaigrette . . . .

¼	cup Red Wine-Garlic Vinaigrette (see page 127)
2	tablespoons dried Italian seasoning

• Prepare the Red Wine-Garlic Vinaigrette.

• Whisk together the vinaigrette and Italian seasoning.

tip   If you want to make this salad ahead of time, toss together everything but the olives and Baby Arugula. Refrigerate until ready to serve.

black-eyed pea salad

Nothing is more southern than the combination of black-eyed peas and greens. For a lighter version, I substituted tender baby spinach leaves for the traditional collard greens. **MAKES 6 SIDE SALADS**

¼	cup Red Wine Vinaigrette (see page 180)
2	cans (15-ounces each) black-eyed peas, rinsed and drained
½	red bell pepper, seeded and finely diced
½	green bell pepper, seeded and finely diced
½	red onion, finely diced
½	jalapeño, seeded and finely diced
1	small garlic clove, minced
	Kosher salt and freshly ground pepper
1	bag (6 ounces) Baby Spinach, coarsely chopped

• Prepare the Red Wine Vinaigrette.

• In a large salad bowl, toss together the black-eyed peas, red bell pepper, green bell pepper, red onion, jalapeño, and garlic. Add the vinaigrette to taste and gently toss to coat. Season with salt and pepper to taste.

• Divide the spinach among the plates. Top with a generous spoonful of the black-eyed pea mixture. Serve immediately.

tip For an authentic southern touch, add a dash of hot sauce to the black-eyed pea mixture for a little extra zing.

edamame garden salad
with citrus-soy vinaigrette

A popular source of protein in Asia for centuries, edamame have recently popped up on menus across the United States. **MAKES 6 APPETIZER OR SIDE SALADS**

salad . . . .

2	cups frozen shelled edamame
1	carrot, peeled and shredded on the large holes of a traditional grater
¼	cup halved and sliced radishes
¼	cup cherry tomatoes, quartered
½	cucumber, halved lengthwise, seeded, and diced
1	bag (5 ounces) Sweet Baby Greens

• Bring a large pot of salted water to a boil. Add the edamame, return to a boil, and cook until just tender, 3 to 5 minutes more. Drain the edamame and rinse with cold water until cooled. Place in a large salad bowl.

• Add the carrot, radishes, tomatoes, cucumber, and Sweet Baby Greens. Add the vinaigrette to taste and gently toss to coat. Serve immediately.

citrus-soy vinaigrette . . . .

3	tablespoons freshly squeezed orange juice
2	tablespoons freshly squeezed lemon juice
2	tablespoons soy sauce
2	tablespoons canola oil
	Kosher salt and freshly ground pepper

• In a small bowl whisk together the orange juice, lemon juice, soy sauce, and oil until well combined. Season with salt and pepper to taste.
MAKES ABOUT ½ CUP

tip   Edamame are soybeans that have been harvested at the peak of ripening. They are sold in your grocery's frozen food section.

green pea salad

Perfect for a hot day, this light and refreshing salad can be made ahead of time.

MAKES 6 APPETIZER OR SIDE SALADS

3	cups frozen green peas, thawed
⅓	cup sour cream
⅓	cup plain yogurt
½	cup thinly sliced scallions
	Kosher salt and freshly ground pepper
1	bag (7 ounces) Riviera™ Blend

• In a large salad bowl, toss together the peas, sour cream, yogurt, and scallions. Season to taste with salt and pepper. Cover and refrigerate until cold.

• Divide the Riviera Blend among individual plates. Top with a generous spoonful of the pea salad.

tip No need to cook the frozen peas since they were parboiled before freezing.

slaws

honey-lime corn slaw

This light and piquant slaw is the perfect accompaniment for Southwest-flavored chicken and meats. I also like to use it to garnish fish tacos. MAKES 6 SIDE SALADS

slaw . . . .

3	ears fresh corn, shucked
1	bag (10 ounces) Angel Hair Cole Slaw
1	red bell pepper, seeded and thinly sliced
2	scallions, thinly sliced
¼	cup fresh cilantro leaves, coarsely chopped
	Kosher salt and freshly ground pepper

• Place the corn in a medium pot of boiling salted water. Cook until tender, about 5 to 6 minutes. Drain, rinse with cold water to stop cooking, and set aside until cool enough to handle. Using a small knife, carefully slice the kernels off the cob; discard the cobs. Place the kernels in a large salad bowl.

• Add the Angel Hair Cole Slaw, red bell pepper, scallions, and cilantro and toss.

• Add the vinaigrette to taste and toss to coat. Season with salt and pepper to taste.

honey-lime vinaigrette . . . .

⅓	cup freshly squeezed lime juice
2	tablespoons honey
3	tablespoons extra-virgin olive oil
	Kosher salt and freshly ground pepper

• In a small bowl whisk together the lime juice, honey, and oil until well combined. Season with salt and pepper to taste. MAKES ABOUT ½ CUP

tip If fresh corn is not available, substitute frozen corn kernels. Frozen corn kernels have a fresher taste and crunchier texture than the canned variety.

To avoid flying kernels, stand the cob upright in the bottom of a deep bowl. Carefully slice the kernels off the cob into the bowl.

creamy broccoli slaw

This multicolored slaw was inspired by the sweet broccoli and raisin salad served at delis. **MAKES 6 SIDE SALADS**

slaw . . . .

1	bag (16 ounces) Broccoli Cole Slaw
½	pound bacon (about 10 slices), cooked and crumbled
½	small red onion, finely chopped
½	cup raisins
⅔	cup toasted sunflower seeds
	Kosher salt and freshly ground pepper

• Place the Broccoli Cole Slaw, bacon, onion, raisins, and sunflower seeds in a large salad bowl. Add the dressing to taste and toss until well coated. Season with salt and pepper to taste.

dressing . . . .

½	cup mayonnaise
3	tablespoons sugar
1½	tablespoons champagne vinegar

• In a small bowl whisk together the mayonnaise, sugar, and champagne vinegar until the sugar has dissolved. MAKES ABOUT ½ CUP

tip Champagne vinegar has a light and mild flavor perfect for dressing a delicately flavored salad. White wine vinegar is a good, but not quite as mild, substitute.

carrot slaw with cumin and cilantro

This refreshing slaw is a great to bring on a picnic. **MAKES 10 SIDE SALADS**

slaw . . . .

1	bag (10 ounces) Shredded Carrots
1	bag (10 ounces) Angel Hair Cole Slaw
1	jalapeño, seeded and minced
6	tablespoons chopped fresh cilantro leaves
	Kosher salt and freshly ground pepper.

• In a large salad bowl, toss together the Shredded Carrots, Angel Hair Cole Slaw, and jalapeño. Drizzle with the dressing to taste and gently toss to coat. Add the cilantro and toss. Season with salt and pepper to taste.

dressing . . . .

¼	cup canola oil
¼	cup freshly squeezed lime juice
1	teaspoon ground cumin

• In a small bowl whisk together the oil, lime juice, and cumin until well combined. MAKES ABOUT ½ CUP

tip Be careful when seeding the jalapeño not to touch your face until all the pepper oils are washed off your hands. If seeding several hot peppers, try wearing disposable gloves to prevent getting "burned" by the oils.

asian slaw with ginger dressing

My husband, Paul, asked me to include a recipe for a Japanese restaurant-style ginger dressing. In my opinion, this tangy dressing is better over crunchy slaw rather than the iceberg lettuce traditionally served at restaurants. Try it and you decide. **MAKES 6 SIDE SALADS**

slaw . . . .

1	bag (16 ounces) 3-Color Deli Cole Slaw
4	scallions, thinly sliced
½	red onion, halved and thinly sliced
1	tablespoon sesame seeds

• In a large salad bowl, toss together the 3-Color Deli Cole Slaw, scallions, red onion, and sesame seeds. Add the dressing to taste and gently toss. Serve immediately.

ginger dressing . . . .

3	tablespoons soy sauce
1	tablespoon freshly squeezed lime juice
3	tablespoons mayonnaise
1	tablespoon grated freshly peeled ginger
1	tablespoon distilled white vinegar
1	tablespoon dark brown sugar
½	teaspoon toasted sesame oil
	Kosher salt and freshly ground pepper

• In a small bowl whisk together the soy sauce, lime juice, mayonnaise, ginger, vinegar, brown sugar, and sesame oil. Season with salt and pepper to taste. MAKES ABOUT ½ CUP

tip Since this salad should be served immediately after it is tossed with the dressing, wait to make it until everything else on your menu is ready.

pink lady apple slaw

My good friend Allyson James came up with this sweet slaw. The fruity dressing is made from apple butter, a highly concentrated form of applesauce produced by slow cooking the apples until they are caramelized. There is no real butter in apple butter; the name refers to its creamy consistency. You can find it in the jams and jellies section of your local grocery. **MAKES 6 SIDE SALADS**

slaw . . . .

1	bag (10 ounce) Angel Hair Cole Slaw
½	cup dried cranberries
1	bunch watercress, stems discarded and leaves coarsely chopped
3	apples (preferably Pink Ladies), cored and sliced into thin strips

• In a large salad bowl, toss together the Angel Hair Cole Slaw, cranberries, watercress, and apples. Add the dressing to taste and gently toss. Serve immediately.

apple butter dressing . . . .

⅓	cup freshly squeezed lime juice
3	tablespoons apple butter
	Kosher salt and freshly ground pepper

• In a small bowl whisk together the lime juice and apple butter. Season with salt and pepper to taste. MAKES ABOUT ⅓ CUP

tip A cross between Golden Delicious and Lady William apples, Pink Lady apples have a sweetly tart flavor and creamy texture. If you can't find them in your local store, substitute Golden Delicious apples and add a pinch of sugar.

crunchy cole slaw

Full of seeds, nuts, and noodles, this slaw has an irresistible crunch. MAKES 6 SIDE SALADS

slaw . . . .

1	bag (10 ounces) Angel Hair Cole Slaw
¼	cup sliced scallions
½	package (3 ounces) plain Ramen noodles, lightly broken
2	tablespoons sesame seeds
3	tablespoons slivered blanched almonds, toasted
2	tablespoons sunflower seeds

• In a large salad bowl, toss together the Angel Hair Cole Slaw, scallions, Ramen noodles, sesame seeds, almonds, and sunflower seeds. Add the dressing to taste and gently toss. Serve immediately.

dressing . . . .

½	cup canola oil
1	tablespoon soy sauce
¼	cup sugar
¼	cup red wine vinegar
	Kosher salt and freshly ground pepper

• In a small bowl whisk together the oil, soy sauce, sugar, and vinegar until the sugar has dissolved. Season with salt and pepper to taste. MAKES ABOUT 1 CUP

tip Toss this salad with the dressing just before serving to keep the nuts and noodles crunchy.

mandarin orange slaw

Fruity, colorful, lots of flavor . . . those are the best words to describe this yummy side dish. **MAKES 6 SIDE SALADS**

slaw . . . .

1	bag (10 ounces) Shredded Red Cabbage
¼	cup sliced scallions
2	carrots, peeled and shaved into ribbons with a vegetable peeler
¼	cup dried cranberries
1	cup drained Mandarin orange slices (available jarred or canned)
¼	cup pine nuts, toasted
	Kosher salt and freshly ground pepper

• In a large salad bowl, toss together the Shredded Red Cabbage, scallions, carrots, cranberries, Mandarin oranges, and pine nuts. Add the dressing to taste and toss to coat. Season with salt and pepper to taste. Serve immediately.

dressing . . . .

¼	cup firmly packed light brown sugar
¼	cup red wine vinegar
2	tablespoons juice from Mandarin orange slices (available jarred or canned)
½	cup vegetable oil

• In a small bowl whisk together the brown sugar, vinegar, and Mandarin orange juice until the sugar has dissolved. Slowly add the oil in a steady stream, whisking to emulsify. MAKES ABOUT 1 CUP

tip Canned or jarred Mandarin orange slices are slices from small, seedless Japanese Satsuma oranges.

oriental vegetable slaw

Full of a myriad of delicious vegetables, this hearty slaw is the only side dish you will need to accompany your main course. An Asian-inspired dish such as Teriyaki chicken or salmon would be the perfect match.

MAKES 6 SIDE SALADS

slaw . . . .

1	cup fresh snow peas
1	bag (10 ounces) Angel Hair Cole Slaw
1	cup drained baby corn (available jarred or canned)
⅔	cup drained marinated straw mushrooms (available jarred or canned)
½	cup chow mein noodles
3	tablespoons black sesame seeds

• Bring salted water to a boil in a medium pot. Add the snow peas and cook until vibrant green and crisp tender, 1 to 1½ minutes. Drain the snow peas and immerse in an ice water bath to stop the cooking process. Drain again and place in a large salad bowl.

• Add the Angel Hair Cole Slaw, baby corn, mushrooms, noodles, and sesame seeds. Add the dressing to taste and gently toss. Serve immediately.

rice vinegar dressing . . . .

¼	cup rice vinegar
¾	teaspoon sesame oil
2	tablespoons peanut oil (substitute canola oil if allergic)
	Kosher salt and freshly ground pepper

• In a small bowl whisk together the vinegar, sesame oil, and peanut oil. Season with salt and pepper to taste. MAKES ABOUT ¼ CUP

tip Feel free to add or substitute your favorite Asian vegetables to this slaw.

carrot salad
with toasted pine nuts

The simple lemon dressing enhances the garden-fresh flavors of the carrots and parsley in this bright salad.
MAKES 4 TO 6 SIDE SALADS

slaw . . . .

1	bag (10 ounces) Shredded Carrots
½	cup pine nuts, toasted (see tip on page 91)
¼	cup coarsely chopped flat-leaf Italian parsley
2	teaspoons minced garlic
	Kosher salt and freshly ground pepper

• In a large salad bowl, toss together the Shredded Carrots, pine nuts, parsley, and garlic. Add the dressing to taste and toss gently. Season with salt and pepper to taste.

dressing . . . .

3	tablespoons extra-virgin olive oil
¼	cup freshly squeezed lemon juice
1	tablespoon white wine vinegar
1	tablespoon sugar

• In a small bowl whisk together oil, lemon juice, vinegar, and sugar until sugar has dissolved.
MAKES ABOUT ½ CUP

tip Freshly minced garlic is always best, but to save time, jarred minced garlic can be a great convenience. Just remember that the jarred garlic has a stronger flavor than fresh garlic. Use less than the recipe states; you can always add more later.

three-ingredient slaw

This simple side dish—it only has 3 main ingredients—goes great with just about any entrée. I like to serve it with grilled barbeque chicken. **MAKES 4 TO 6 SIDE SALADS**

slaw . . . .

1	bag (10 ounces) Angel Hair Cole Slaw
½	cup sliced scallions
¼	cup coarsely chopped fresh parsley leaves
	Kosher salt and freshly ground pepper

• In a large salad bowl, toss together the Angel Hair Cole Slaw, scallions, and parsley. Add the dressing to taste and gently toss. Season with salt and pepper to taste.

dressing . . . .

¼	cup mayonnaise
½	cup sour cream
1	tablespoon honey mustard
1½	teaspoons white wine vinegar
½	teaspoon granulated sugar
	Kosher salt and freshly ground pepper

• In a small bowl whisk together the mayonnaise, sour cream, honey mustard, vinegar, and sugar until the sugar has dissolved. Season with salt and pepper to taste. MAKES ABOUT ¾ CUP

tip Both flat-leaf Italian parsley and curly-leaf parsley add a bright, fresh flavor to a dish. Flat-leaf parsley has a stronger flavor than its curly-leaf counterpart. It also tends to hold up better in the cooking process.

old-fashioned cole slaw
with buttermilk dressing

For those who love a classic, this creamy slaw with tangy buttermilk dressing is sure to please.
MAKES 6 SIDE SALADS

slaw . . . .

1	bag (16 ounces) 3-Color Deli Cole Slaw

• In a large salad bowl, toss together the 3-Color Deli Cole Slaw and dressing to taste. Refrigerate until ready to serve.

buttermilk dressing . . . .

½	cup reduced-fat buttermilk
2	tablespoons mayonnaise
2	tablespoons sour cream
1	shallot, minced
½	teaspoon cider vinegar
¼	teaspoon Dijon mustard
1	teaspoon granulated sugar
	Kosher salt and freshly ground pepper

• In a small bowl whisk together the buttermilk, mayonnaise, sour cream, shallot, vinegar, mustard, and sugar until the sugar has dissolved. Season with salt and pepper to taste. MAKES ABOUT ¾ CUP

memphis mustard cole slaw

Down in Memphis, folks prefer a tangy mustard cole slaw with their barbeque rather than the traditional mayonnaise variety. MAKES 6 SIDE SALADS

slaw . . . .

1	bag (16 ounces) Classic Cole Slaw
½	green bell pepper, seeded and finely chopped
2	tablespoons celery seed
	Hot sauce

• In a large salad bowl, toss together the Classic Cole Slaw, green bell pepper, and celery seed. Add the dressing to taste and gently toss until well combined. Season with hot sauce to taste.

dressing . . . .

¼	cup prepared yellow mustard
¼	cup apple cider vinegar
½	cup freshly squeezed lemon juice
1½	cups sugar
	Kosher salt and freshly ground pepper

• In small bowl whisk together the mustard, vinegar, lemon juice, and sugar until the sugar has dissolved. Season with salt and pepper to taste.
MAKES ABOUT 2 CUPS

dieter's slaw

Dieting or not, this flavorful slaw makes a great side dish. **MAKES 6 SIDE SALADS**

slaw . . . .

1   bag (16 ounces) 3-Color Deli Cole Slaw

• In a large salad bowl, toss the 3-Color Deli Cole Slaw with the dressing to taste. Refrigerate for at least 1 hour before serving to let the dressing marinate the slaw.

low-fat cider vinegar dressing . . . .

½   cup apple cider vinegar
¼   cup water
1   cup Splenda
1   teaspoon celery seeds

• In a medium sauce pan bring the vinegar, water, Splenda, and celery seeds to a boil. Cook until the Splenda has dissolved, about 1 minute. Remove from the heat and cool to room temperature, about 30 minutes. **MAKES ABOUT ¾ CUP**

tip Transfer the hot dressing to a bowl to cool faster.

vinaigrettes & dressings

basic vinaigrette

This is the basic formula for all vinaigrettes—1 part vinegar to 3 parts oil. If you prefer a more tart vinaigrette, alter the ratio to equal parts vinegar to oil. Substitute your favorite vinegar or oil as desired.
MAKES ABOUT ¼ CUP

2   tablespoons white wine vinegar
6   tablespoons extra-virgin olive oil
      Kosher salt and freshly ground pepper

• Place the vinegar in a small bowl and whisk together. Slowly add the oil in a stream, whisking to emulsify. Season with salt and pepper to taste.

tip   To emulsify a vinaigrette means to combine two liquids, oil and vinegar, that normally do not mix smoothly. This is done by slowly adding one ingredient to another while whisking rapidly. Emulsifying disperses and suspends one liquid throughout another. If your vinaigrette separates, just whisk it back together.

Vinaigrettes keep in the refrigerator for up to two weeks. Since the oil and vinega will separate, just whisk it to re-emulsify. I like to store my dressings in a glass jar; to re-emulsify all I need to do is shake vigorously. If the oil has solidified, let the vinaigrette come back to room temperature before re-emulsifying.

balsamic grainy mustard vinaigrette

I just love the flavor and texture that whole-grain mustard gives to this dressing. Try substituting white balsamic vinegar or white wine vinegar. **MAKES ABOUT ¼ CUP**

2	tablespoons balsamic vinegar
1	tablespoon whole-grain Dijon mustard
6	tablespoons extra-virgin olive oil
	Kosher salt and freshly ground pepper

• Place the vinegar and mustard in a small bowl and whisk together. Slowly add the oil in a stream, whisking to emulsify. Season with salt and pepper to taste.

tip   This recipe is the basis of all mustard vinaigrettes. If you prefer a smoother texture, use traditional Dijon mustard in place of the whole-grain variety.

garlic vinaigrette

Calling all garlic lovers! MAKES ABOUT ¼ CUP

excellent.

½	small garlic clove, mashed to a paste or minced
1	teaspoon Dijon mustard
2	tablespoons white wine vinegar
6	tablespoons extra-virgin olive oil
	Kosher salt and freshly ground pepper

• Place the garlic in the bottom of a small bowl. Blend in the mustard and vinegar. Slowly add the oil in a stream, whisking to emulsify. Season with salt and pepper to taste.

tip To best incorporate that wonderful garlic flavor into a dressing, the garlic should be mashed to a paste. Place the garlic in a mortar with a pinch of kosher salt and use the pestle to mash it together until you have a paste. If you don't have a mortar and pestle, place the garlic and a pinch of salt on a cutting board and mince the garlic with a sharp knife until a paste is formed. A third option is to use a garlic press to crush the garlic.

Unlike traditional vinaigrettes, vinaigrettes made with fresh garlic should not be stored. Garlic can quickly turn oil rancid.

lemon vinaigrette

A vinaigrette is any dressing made from oil and an acid such as vinegar or citrus juice. Freshly squeezed lemon juice gives this vinaigrette a lighter and brighter flavor than its vinegar-based cousins. **MAKES ABOUT ¼ CUP**

2	tablespoons freshly squeezed lemon juice
1	tablespoon Dijon mustard
6	tablespoons extra-virgin olive oil
	Kosher salt and freshly ground pepper

• In a small bowl whisk together the lemon juice and mustard. Slowly add the oil in a stream, whisking to emulsify. Season with salt and pepper to taste.

tip Only use freshly squeezed lemon or lime juice when making a vinaigrette. The bottled version does not have the same bright, citrus flavor.

buttermilk ranch dressing

Ranch is a classic American favorite. Buttermilk adds an appealing tangy flavor to this creamy dressing.
MAKES ABOUT ³/₄ CUP

½	cup buttermilk
¼	cup mayonnaise
1	tablespoon sour cream
¼	teaspoon apple cider vinegar
½	teaspoon minced garlic
⅛	teaspoon dry mustard
¼	teaspoon dried thyme
1	tablespoon finely chopped fresh chives
	Kosher salt and freshly ground pepper

• In a small bowl whisk together the buttermilk, mayonnaise, sour cream, vinegar, garlic, dry mustard, thyme, and chives. Season with salt and pepper to taste. Refrigerate until ready to use.

thousand island dressing

This thick and rich dressing, often served as a condiment for sandwiches, is best served over a heartier salad blend such as Hearts of Romaine or American Blend. Tried and true, this version is from my good friend Alison Foster's grandmother. **MAKES ABOUT 1 CUP**

½	cup mayonnaise
2	tablespoons pickle relish
1	hard-boiled egg, peeled and grated
½	teaspoon Worcestershire sauce
2	tablespoons chili sauce
1	teaspoon freshly squeezed lemon juice
	Kosher salt and freshly ground pepper
	Dash of Tabasco (optional)

• In a small bowl whisk together the mayonnaise, relish, egg, Worcestershire sauce, chili sauce, and lemon juice until well combined. Season to taste with salt, pepper, and Tabasco, if using.

tip Many Thousand Island dressing recipes call for ketchup as opposed to chili sauce. I think the chili sauce gives the dressing more complexity.

233

peanut dressing

Traditionally served on Asian-inspired salads, I find the sweet and creamy flavor of peanut dressings irresistible.
MAKES ABOUT 1 CUP

¼	cup rice wine vinegar
2	tablespoons creamy peanut butter
1	teaspoon finely grated freshly peeled ginger
1	tablespoon soy sauce
1	tablespoon honey
2	teaspoons toasted sesame oil
½	cup canola oil
	Pinch of red pepper flakes (optional)
	Kosher salt and freshly ground pepper

• In a small bowl whisk together the vinegar, peanut butter, ginger, soy sauce, honey, sesame oil, canola oil, and red pepper flakes. Season with salt and pepper to taste.

tip If you use natural peanut butter, you may need to add a little sugar to sweeten the flavor.

many thanks

My wonderful family, I am forever indebted to you for your support and understanding as I pursue my dreams. This book would never have happened it weren't for you.

Paul, thank you for always putting up with me, never complaining about eating salad every night for dinner, and being my inspiration.

Hannah and Sarah, thanks for all your giggles, hugs, and kisses.

Mom and Dad, for understanding and supporting me oh so many years ago when I decided to pack up my bags, move to France, and go to culinary school

Dad, for giving me your passion for cooking and enjoying good food.

Mom, thanks for allowing your home to be turned into a photo studio and being the grandmother-extraordinaire taking care of the girls while I worked.

Susan, thanks for generously editing my book, finding ingredients out of season, and staying on the phone with me for hours testing recipes together. You are the best.

Rollin Riggs and Melissa Ellis, for sharing your publishing expertise.

Allison Lemm, for being a generous friend and proofreading my book.

Babcock's Gifts and Macy's, for sharing your fantastic dishes and linens to make the salads look perfect.

Gina Bartz, for all those hours helping me pick just the right plate.

To all those who shared recipes, tested recipes, and lent me plates . . . especially Lucia Heros, Allyson James, Ashley Woodman, Maritucker Hanemann, Fontaine Brown, Nick and Jenny

Vergos, Alison Foster, May Weiss, Amy Pearce, Stephanie Linkous, Andrea Bordwell, and Beth Murrey.

Maria, for being a wonderful mother-in-law and watching my girls whenever I needed your help.

Langdon Clay, for making this book beautiful with your stunning photography.

Larry Stone, Geoffrey Stone, Bryan Curtis and all the folks at Rutledge Hill Press, who helped bring this book to life.

Ellen Rolfes, thank you for believing in me. Without your recommendation, this book would not have happened.

credits

Unless otherwise noted, tableware shown in photographs is privately owned.

GREEN SALADS:

Steakhouse Wedge Salad with Bacon, Tomatoes, and Blue Cheese: *Plate and placemat from Babcock's Gifts*

Asian Salad with Ponzu Ginger Dressing and Wasabi Peas: *Plate and napkin from Babcock's Gifts*

Arugula with Shaved Parmesan: *Bowl and placemat from Babcock's Gifts*

Warm Goat Cheese Salad with Grainy Mustard Vinaigrette: *Plate from Babcock's Gifts*

Southern Caesar Salad with Roasted Garlic Dressing: *Plate, linens, and fork from Babcock's Gifts*

Spinach Salad with Roasted Cherry Tomatoes: *Plate, linens, and fork from Babcock's Gifts*

Classic Spinach Salad with Bacon, Red Onion, and Hard-Boiled Eggs: *Bowl, plate, and linens from Babcock's Gifts*

Classic Caesar Salad with Herb Croutons: *Bowl and plate from Babcock's Gifts*

Hot Chili Oil Salad: *Plate from Babcock's Gifts*

Grilled Romaine with Green Goddess Dressing: *Plate from Babcock's Gifts*

POULTRY SALADS:

Chinese Chicken Salad with Peanut Dressing: *Plate from Babcock's Gifts*

Mandarin Chicken Salad with Toasted Sesame Vinaigrette: *Plate from Babcock's Gifts*

Margarita Chicken Salad with Pepitas, Cranberries, and Cojita Cheese: *Plate and linens from Babcock's Gifts*

Cobb Salad with Buttermilk Garlic Dressing: *Bowl from Babcock's Gifts*

Chicken Stir-Fry Salad: *Plate from Macy's*

BBQ Chicken Salad with Black Bean and Corn Salsa: *Plate from Babcock's Gifts*

Chicken Tostada Salad with Salsa Verde: *Plate from Babcock's Gifts*

Orange Chicken over Mixed Greens with Citrus Vinaigrette: *Plate from Babcock's Gifts*

Chicken Paillard topped with Fresh Greens: *Plate from Babcock's Gifts*
Chicken Florentine Salad: *Plate from Babcock's Gifts*

MEAT SALADS:

Grilled Steak Salad with Marinated Mushrooms, Blue Cheese Crumbles, and Red Onion: *Plate from Babcock's Gifts*
BLT Salad: *Plate from Babcock's Gifts*
Taco Salad: *Bowl and plate from Babcock's Gifts*
Italian Chef Salad: *Bowl and linens from Babcock's Gifts*
Thai Beef Salad: *Plate and placemat from Babcock's Gifts*
Antipasti Platter: *Platter and tablecloth from Babcock's Gifts*
Grilled Pork Tenderloin Salad with Apricot Balsamic Vinaigrette: *Plate and placemat from Babcock's Gifts*
Prosciutto and Melon Salad: *Plate and placemat from Babcock's Gifts*
Beef Tenderloin with Mâche: *Plate, placemat, and linens from Babcock's Gifts*
Grilled Lamb and Tabbouleh Salad: *Plate and linens from Babcock's Gifts*
Fajita Salad: *Bowl and plate from Babcock's Gifts*

SEAFOOD SALADS:

Seared Salmon over Mixed Greens with Dried Cranberries, Feta Cheese, and Candied Pecans: *Plate and placemat from Babcock's Gifts*
Tuna Niçoise: *Bowl, plate, and napkin from Babcock's Gifts*
Salmon and Asparagus Salad with Pesto Vinaigrette: *Plate and linens from Babcock's Gifts*
Butter Lettuce tossed with Smoked Salmon, Capers, and Dill: *Plate from Babcock's Gifts*
Seared Tuna Salad with Honey-Lime Cilantro Dressing: *Plate and placemat from Babcock's Gifts*
Shrimp tossed with Herb Salad and Lemony-Ginger Vinaigrette: *Plate and linens from Babcock's Gifts*
Shrimp Stir-Fry Salad: *Bowl from Macy's and Charger from Babcock's Gifts*
Lobster Salad with Grapefruit Vinaigrette: *Plate and placemat from Babcock's Gifts*
Crawfish Salad with Spicy Cajun Remoulade: *Bowl and linens from Babcock's Gifts*
Spanish Shrimp, Orange, and Olive Salad: *Plate from Babcock's Gifts*
Maryland Crab Cake Salad with Caper Remoulade: *Plate from Babcock's Gifts*

VEGGIE SALADS:

Warm Fingerling Potato Salad with Bacon and Croutons: *Bowl from Babcock's Gifts*

Greek Salad: *Plate from Babcock's Gifts*

Asparagus, Roasted Red Pepper, and Arugula Salad: *Plate from Babcock's Gifts*

Layered Chop Salad: *Glass compote and linens from Babcock's Gifts*

Caprese Salad: *Plate and linens from Babcock's Gifts*

Summer Vegetable Salad: *Plate and linens from Babcock's Gifts*

Meze-in-a-Minute Platter: *Platter from Babcock's Gifts*

Crunchy Asian Salad: *Plate from Babcock's Gifts*

Insalata Primavera: *Bowl from Babcock's Gifts*

Grilled Vegetable Salad: *Plate from Macy's*

Hearts of Palm Salad with Red Onion Vinaigrette: *Plate from Babcock's Gifts*

FRUIT SALADS:

Mango, Avocado, and Cilantro Salad: *Plate and placemat from Babcock's Gifts*

English Farmhouse Salad: *Bowl from Babcock's Gifts*

Balsamic Strawberry Salad: *Plate and linens from Babcock's Gifts*

Pear and Spinach Salad: *Plate from Babcock's Gifts*

Orange and Fennel Salad: *Plate from Babcock's Gifts*

Watermelon and Arugula Salad: *Bowl and placemat from Babcock's Gifts*

Grapefruit and Avocado Salad: *Plate from Babcock's Gifts*

Arugula with Goat Cheese-Stuffed Figs and Fig Vinaigrette: *Plates from Macy's*

Waldorf Salad: *Bowl, napkin, and placemat from Babcock's Gifts*

Fresh Fruit Salad with Poppy Seed Dressing: *Plate from Macy's*

Hearts of Romaine with Tart Apples, Hazelnuts, and Sharp Cheddar Cheese: *Plate and napkin from Babcock's Gifts*

Mixed Lettuces with Strawberries, Red Grapes, and Almonds: *Plate from Babcock's Gifts*

Tropical Fruit Salad with Passion Fruit Vinaigrette: *Plate from Babcock's Gifts and Napkin from Macy's*

BEANS, GRAINS, RICE & PASTA:

Cheese Tortellini Salad with Sun-Dried Tomato Vinaigrette: *Bowl from Babcock's Gifts*

Lentil and Tri-Color Pepper Salad: *Plates from Macy's*

Brown Rice, Corn, and Grilled Vegetable Salad: *Bowl from Macy's*

Cannellini Bean and Roasted Red Pepper Salad: *Plate and placemat from Babcock's Gifts*

Curried Rice and Chickpea Salad: *Plate from Macy's*

Grilled Portobello and Couscous Salad: *Plate from Macy's*

Mediterranean Pasta Salad: *Bowl from Macy's*

Edamame Garden Salad with Citrus-Soy Vinaigrette: *Bowl from Macy's*

Green Pea Salad: *Plate from Babcock's Gifts*

SLAWS:

Honey-Lime Corn Slaw: *Plate and linens from Babcock's Gifts*

Creamy Broccoli Slaw: *Plate from Babcock's Gifts*

Carrot Slaw with Cumin and Cilantro: *Plate from Babcock's Gifts*

Asian Slaw with Ginger Dressing: *Plate from Babcock's Gifts*

Crunchy Cole Slaw: *Plate from Babcock's Gifts*

Mandarin Orange Slaw: *Plate from Babcock's Gifts*

Oriental Vegetable Slaw: *Plate and linens from Babcock's Gifts*

Carrot Salad with Toasted Pine Nuts: *Plate from Babcock's Gifts*

Three-Ingredient Slaw: *Plate from Babcock's Gifts*

Memphis Mustard Cole Slaw: *Plate from Babcock's Gifts*

Dieter's Slaw: *Bowl and plate from Macy's*

index